Lost World of the Aegean

The Emergence of Man

Lost World of the Aegean

by Maitland A. Edey
and the Editors
of Time-Life Books

Time-Life Books
New York

The Author: MAITLAND A. EDEY retired as editor of TIME-LIFE
BOOKS in 1970 in order to write books himself. Since then he
has written four: *The Northeast Coast* in The American Wil-
derness series, *The Missing Link* and *The Sea Traders* in The
Emergence of Man series, and now this book on the Bronze
Age Aegean. He is also the author of *The Cats of Africa* and
two books on ornithology, *American Songbirds* and *American Waterbirds.*

The Consultants: COLIN RENFREW, Professor of Archaeology
at the University of Southampton, England, has excavated several prehistoric sites in Greece, and in his book, *The
Emergence of Civilisation,* analyzed the developments of culture in the Cyclades, Crete and Greece during the Third
Millennium B.C. He is an expert on radiocarbon dating, and
has written a definitive work on the subject: *Before Civilization.* He is also a specialist in the origins of society in Western Europe and in the beginnings of trade there. JOSEPH
WINTERBOTHAM SHAW is Associate Professor of Fine Art at
the University of Toronto and is Research Associate in the
Greek and Roman Department of the Royal Ontario Museum.
He has been archeologically active for years in Greece and
elsewhere in the Mediterranean. His main interest lies in Minoan Crete, where he has worked primarily at Kato Zakro
and Knossos. His recently published book, *Minoan Architecture: Materials and Techniques,* is the first complete study of
the methods of construction and the building materials uti-
lized in Minoan architecture.

The Cover: Lounging at the light well by the grand staircase
of the palace at Knossos, two ladies of the Minoan royal
court idle with a pet monkey imported from North Africa.
The scene—set at the peak of Minoan civilization, between
1600 and 1500 B.C.—was painted true to life by artist Michael
A. Hampshire. He superimposed the ladies on a photograph
of the eastern wing of the palace as it looks today, some 70
years after it was restored by archeologist Arthur Evans.

Contents

Introduction

As recently as a century ago, the history of the Western world began with Classical Greece and ancient Rome. No one dreamed that, a thousand years before the poetry of Homer or the philosophy of Plato, there flourished in Greece and on Crete a brilliant civilization, a world of citadels and palaces, of warriors and scribes, of painters and goldsmiths, which the new science of archeology in a series of dramatic discoveries would soon recover and restore. The impressive palaces of Crete—with their spacious courts and labyrinthine passages, centers of a culture we now call Minoan—still lay unsuspected beneath the earth. The golden treasures, still buried after more than 3,000 years in the warrior graves of Mycenae, had yet to give their name to the Mycenaean civilization, which today we regard as the direct ancestor of the Classical Greek world.

This book tells with clarity and vividness how a century of excavation and research has re-created that vanished world of the Cycladic islands, Minoan Crete and Mycenaean Greece. Archeology has reconstructed a way of life that even in Homer's time, less than 500 years later, was only a shadowy recollection. Indeed today we can look on the very bronze swords and daggers and those same golden drinking cups that Homer, relying on tradition, described—although he probably never actually saw one himself. We can walk into the citadel at Mycenae and enter the great, stone, vaulted tombs where its princes were laid to rest. We can stroll across the spacious central court at the palace of King Minos on Crete, count the storage jars in his palace magazines and admire the décor in his throne room. Most remarkable of all, we can walk the streets of volcanic Thera, the island destroyed in a colossal eruption around 1500 B.C., and see the pottery and the frescoes —unearthed in just the past few years—whose lively themes make real a world that for millennia had lain forgotten.

Forgotten, but not dead, for in a sense many of its technical achievements persisted into Classical Greek times. And we in the West—the inheritors of the Greek tradition—are still affected by them. That is why our interest in the lost world of the Aegean goes beyond the normal fascination with man's evolution and assumes a sharper, personal focus, centering on the origins and ancestry of our own culture and way of life.

Today, however, we cannot discuss the beginnings or the needs of any early civilization without stumbling upon more general and fundamental questions. How and why does a complex, highly organized society emerge at a particular time and place where formerly life and culture were very much simpler? What hidden processes lead to achievements so striking that they continue to impress us more than 3,000 years later? And why are civilizations fated to decline and collapse? What population pressures, what problems of resources, what ecological changes or social stresses worked together to bring about the end of the brilliant age with which this volume deals? These are questions difficult to answer—for any society—even in the modern world. Yet the cultures of the past, as recovered by the techniques of modern archeology, can serve as a kind of laboratory for the study of such processes. Although this discipline is still in its infancy, there is an increasing feeling today that the deeper understanding of the past has a relevance for our own present and future, and should also clarify some of our current problems of overpopulation, pollution and ecological catastrophe. Such general questions underlie much that is written in this book, with its deliberate search to analyze the causes of change.

COLIN RENFREW
Professor of Archaeology
University of Southampton, England

Chapter One: Long Before Homer

In the spring flowers carpet the meadows by the Aegean Sea. They burst out of cracks in the rocks. They flame in the narrow island valleys, and their perfume rolls down the hills and out across the water. Fishermen, kept ashore during the winter storms, launch their boats and go to sea again, just as they were doing 5,000 years ago.

Five thousand years ago. The mysterious yeast that occasionally works to form a civilization from small scattered groups of people with a low level of culture was just beginning to ferment on the Greek mainland and its adjacent islands. A great civilization already existed in Egypt and an even older one in the Tigris-Euphrates Valley. Now a third civilization was about to bloom in the Aegean. This book is about that blooming. It covers the period of the so-called Bronze Age in the Aegean, which ran from approximately 3000 B.C. to 1100 B.C. Then, though the Aegean peoples themselves lived on, their culture vanished as mysteriously as it started, some 400 years before the birth of what most of us recognize today as "ancient"—or Classical—Greece.

Modern knowledge of the Bronze Age Aegean is bafflingly incomplete and surprisingly recent. The antiquity of the Egyptian civilization has long been known, together with the splendor of its art and architecture. By contrast, the Bronze Age in the Aegean was a blank until about a century ago. Filling it in is not unlike assembling the pieces of a jigsaw puzzle

Much of the Cretan coast, like this northeast section with the island of Mochlos in the background, is steep and rocky. In early Minoan times Mochlos was attached to the shore, and ships anchored on its far side were sheltered from the prevailing northwest winds. The enterprising sea traders from there journeyed as far away as Palestine and Egypt.

—pieces that are handed out sparingly as archeologists dig them, one by one, out of the ground. As a result, the picture has not fallen into place smoothly and evenly. Many false assumptions have had to be corrected as new pieces were found. That process is still going on. In fact, during the past couple of decades it has accelerated.

As a starter, all ideas about the Bronze Age Aegean had to be fitted to the references to it that have survived from Classical literature and history. It was generally accepted that the forebears of the Classical Greeks had lived for a long time on the Greek mainland, on Crete and on the other islands of the Aegean. But who these people were or how they lived was not known. That they were the creators of a brilliant—and later lost—civilization was not suspected, not even by the Classical Greeks themselves. Their knowledge of the past—of their own origins—was derived from myth, most of it embalmed in two great epic poems by Homer: the *Iliad* and the *Odyssey*.

In fact the Classical Greeks, though they believed implicitly in Homer and regarded him as their principal historical source, did not really know who he was, where he came from or exactly when he lived. Nor do we today. Modern scholarship recognizes him as a bard (his work that of perhaps two, perhaps several bards), probably illiterate, a teller of ancestral tales inherited from other bards. These he memorized, then reworked to his own taste and sang to his royal patrons. The *Iliad* is an account of a large-scale Greek naval expedition and siege against the fortified city of Troy (Ilios to the Greeks). The *Odyssey* deals with the adventures of one of the Greek warriors, Odysseus, during his attempts to get home again after the sack of Troy.

Homer lived before 700 B.C., but the events that he recited were from an even earlier age, mistily remembered. By the time they were orally handed down to him, they were already heavily glamorized and distorted, having passed through the brains and the mouths of other bards during a period of several hundred years. Thus—and despite the high regard the Classical Greeks had for him—using Homer as a source for real historical events is tricky. The characters in his poems have become mythic creatures—the grandsons of gods, the lovers of goddesses. They are heroes, supermen in magnificently worked armor who fight great battles for great treasure and storm turreted cities. They walk in a world populated by giants, by water nymphs and enchantresses.

Was there any truth at all in Homer's poems? If so, where were his heroes buried? Where were their cities, their armor, their gold? Where did the great Greek leaders—Agamemnon, Menelaus, Odysseus, Nestor —come from? Was there really such a place as Troy?

No one knew. The Greek Achilles and the Trojan Hector danced on the far rim of a dream world, as elusive and as unreal as the giants and nymphs and gods who danced there with them. So it is not surprising that, with the birth of archeology as a scientific tool in unraveling the past, scholars should have come to regard Homer with increasing skepticism as a mere yarn spinner. His stories were fascinating but, though believed by his contemporaries and descendants, they could not be expected to survive unquestioned into modern times. They could no more be taken seriously than Zeus himself—who in Greek myth appeared one minute as a bull, another as a cuckoo, another as a swan, to ravish whatever beautiful woman caught his eye. (Why, one wonders, did Zeus

bother? After all, he *was* Zeus, carrying a fistful of thunderbolts, the most powerful and magnificent male symbol that the human fancy could create. He was overwhelming, unstoppable. Why did he not have his way simply by appearing out of a puff of smoke as—Zeus?)

Take Homer literally? Who could?

One who could was an eccentric German business tycoon and lifelong Homer buff named Heinrich Schliemann. He had made all the money he thought he would ever need and, in 1868, foot-loose and approaching 50, he decided that he would invest some of his wealth in trying to prove a theory he had become seized with: that Homer was talking about things that actually happened. In short, that there was a Troy somewhere. He would find it, and possibly the tombs, the ashes, the armor, the marble palaces and the gold—especially the gold—of its builders. He would search along the northern Aegean coast of modern Turkey just south of the Dardanelles, where long tradition said Troy had been located.

People had wondered about Troy, of course, and some of them had even gone looking for it. Forgetting all the Homeric rubbish about Paris and Helen, they sensibly decided that it was probably a stronghold located near the entrance to the Hellespont, where its rulers could grow rich on the tribute they exacted from traders going back and forth between the Aegean and the Black Sea. In the area there were a couple of tells—earth mounds—each one several acres in size, marking the sites of ancient cities. One tell, named Hissarlik, had caught the interest of an English scholar early in the 19th Century, but he was dead and his ideas had been buried with him. By the time Schliemann became interested in Hissarlik, half of it was owned by another Englishman living in Constantinople. But that gentleman was too busy acting as a consular official to do anything of consequence with it. The other owners were Turks who thought nothing about Homer and cared less. So Hissarlik slumbered in the sun as it had for centuries, its spring flowers nibbled by goats. If there was a Troy anywhere thereabouts, said the experts, it was probably at Bunarbashi—another tell about five miles away from Hissarlik, and farther inland.

Schliemann did not agree. He carried a tattered copy of the *Iliad* with him wherever he went, and read it constantly. He reasoned that if, as the *Iliad* said, the Greek invaders were forever trotting back and forth between Troy and their camp on the seashore, making several trips a day, Troy had to be nearer the water than Bunarbashi. He made contact with the British gentleman in Constantinople. Then, organizing a force of local workmen and not bothering to inform the Turkish owners of the other half of the site, he began to dig at Hissarlik.

He found Troy. In fact, he found nine Troys, a layer cake of cities stacked one over another. During several separate expeditions he found ruined walls of immense stone blocks. He found broken pottery, he found spear tips, stone weapons, huge clay jars as tall as a man, much evidence of fire and destruction. He found King Priam's palace (he thought) and finally (he thought) Priam's treasure: a hoard of silver vases and knives, gold diadems, earrings, and more than 8,000 gold rings and buttons. This treasure he smuggled out of Turkey and, in time, turned over to the German government. Some 70 years later, during the occupation of Nazi Germany by Soviet troops in World War II, the collection disappeared from Berlin. Whether it is still intact somewhere or whether it was melted down and disposed of by ignorant looters is not known. Each passing year makes the latter possibility more probable—a tragedy, for Priam's diadems are among the rarest and most precious artifacts in the entire world.

Schliemann was a secretive man, convinced that others were out to cheat him and therefore not above cheating them. Controversy followed him wherever he went—arguments with governments, with scholars. The experts laughed at him for his windy claims about Priam—and, as it turned out, with justification. In later years, when they got around to investigating Hissarlik themselves, they found that Schliemann had it all wrong. Of the nine layers, the layer he thought was Homeric—Troy II, next to the bottom —turned out to be far older, dating from before 2000 B.C. Troy II had been smashed and consumed in a great fire that Schliemann took to be proof of the wrath of the invading Greeks. In his feverish search for gold, Schliemann had dug helter-skelter right down through what is now conceded to have been Homeric Troy, Troy VII, dating from about 1250 B.C. —without paying any attention to it at all.

For more than 10 years Schliemann worked off and on at Hissarlik, crisscrossing it with trenches. Although he made subsequent smaller finds, he never matched his first great strike of Priam's treasure. Meanwhile he had transferred the focus of his interest to Mycenae on the Greek mainland.

At Mycenae, the situation was somewhat different. Myth and fact seemed to support each other better. There was a ruined citadel at Mycenae, the remains of a fortified city from the remote past, its walls built of huge Cyclopean stones even larger than

The Bronze Age civilizations of the Aegean—enriched by internal contact, isolated from foreign interference—flourished in a compact area

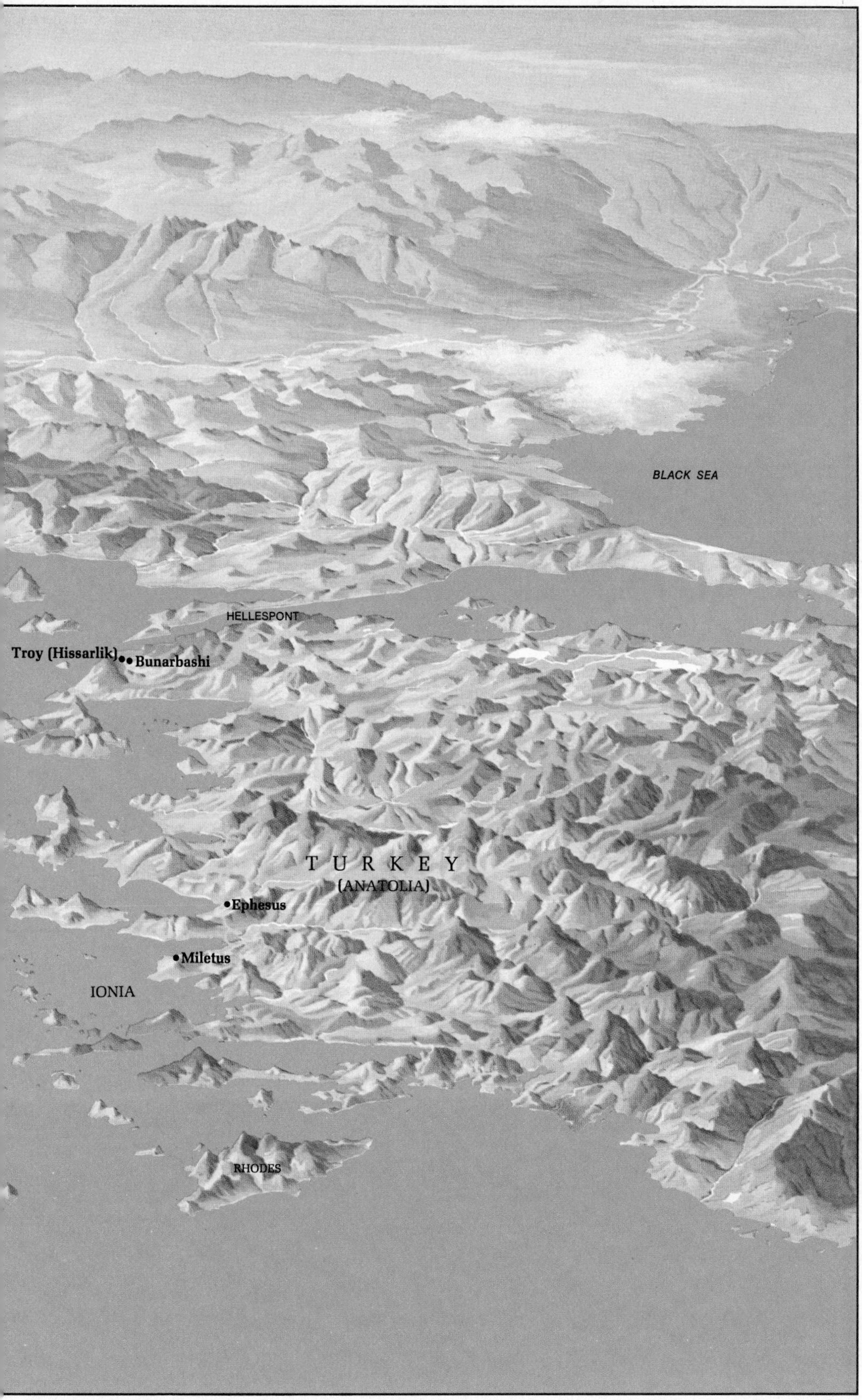

BLACK SEA

HELLESPONT

Troy (Hissarlik) • • Bunarbashi

T U R K E Y
(ANATOLIA)

• Ephesus

• Miletus

IONIA

RHODES

bounded on the south by Crete and, in other directions, by Greece and the Cycladic islands.

The Sea-girt World of the Minoans and Mycenaeans

The Aegean basin is a mountainous region that has not settled down geologically. There is an active volcano on Thera. More than once in recent decades earthquakes have devastated Turkey and northern Greece. Crete was so quake-prone throughout the Bronze Age that builders of the day made allowances for earth tremors in their construction techniques.

In spite of this physical instability, elaborate cultures developed first on the Cycladic islands, then on Crete and finally on the Greek mainland. The accompanying map demonstrates how easy it was—once reliable ships were developed—to populate the islands, and how easily the cultures of the Cyclades could have been swamped after about 1700 B.C. by more powerful influences from larger Crete. The crowding of archeological sites in the Peloponnesus and in Attica has revealed where the main Mycenaean upthrust was centered. From there the Mycenaean Greeks —shortly after 1600 B.C.—encroached on the islands, occupied Crete and finally penetrated eastward to Rhodes, Miletus and Ephesus. By 1250 B.C. there were Greeks throughout the Aegean. They traded and fought with small local kings along the Ionian coast, even got as far as Troy, and succeeded in breaching that stout citadel before their society collapsed, turning the Aegean into a world of darkness and ignorance for 400 years.

those Schliemann had found at Troy. Throughout Greek Classical literature, and down to modern times, Mycenae had been associated with the Greek side of the Trojan legend—with the heroes who had sailed off to fight at Troy under Agamemnon's leadership. The King of Mycenae at that time, according to Classical lore, was Agamemnon, the richest and most powerful ruler in Greece. It was Agamemnon's brother, Menelaus, King of Sparta, who had suffered the humiliation of having his wife Helen stolen by a young seducer from Troy, King Priam's son Paris. That humiliation, according to Homer, had sent the Greeks off in their warships to Troy.

If one believed Homer, and no one did more fervently than Schliemann, then should not one dig at Mycenae for traces of Agamemnon, and for Agamemnon's reputedly immense treasure?

Schliemann dug again and, unbelievably, again struck gold. Within the walls of Mycenae, underneath what appeared to be a circular meeting place or council area paved with stone slabs, he found five royal grave sites containing a number of skeletons and stuffed with an incredible hoard of gold and bronze objects. There were buttons, ornaments, earrings, goblets, vases, sword handles, diadems, necklaces, hundreds and hundreds of thin gold sheets cut into fantastic shapes: leaves, flowers, butterflies, octopuses, stars. And there were masks: masks of gold, some of them stylized, others apparently portraits of dead kings. One mask, Schliemann claimed, was in place on the face of a man in a golden breastplate—a face whose flesh had not yet entirely disappeared.

Bursting with excitement, Schliemann persuaded himself that he recognized the features of this decaying corpse. He notified the Greek government that he had found the grave, the body and the death mask of Agamemnon, together with the remains of Clytemnestra, his wife.

According to Homer and the Greek tragedians, Clytemnestra had taken a lover while her husband was off fighting at Troy. When Agamemnon came home, the lover, Aegisthus, murdered the King and took his throne. Then Clytemnestra's son also returned and avenged his father's death by killing his faithless mother and her paramour.

Schliemann insisted that his excavations had proved the truth of that legend. There was Agamemnon, laid out in all his finery, his body sprinkled with delicate leaves of hammered gold. And there, according to Schliemann, were Clytemnestra and the members of her court, slaughtered on the spot and buried in their turn.

While there is no denying Schliemann's perspicacity—and luck—in making this second fantastic gold strike, his conclusions about it again must be disputed. There was no way of identifying any of the royal remains he unearthed. Almost certainly none was Agamemnon, for the things Schliemann found at Mycenae, just as at Hissarlik, were far older than he thought. Thanks to modern archeology, it is now known that his discoveries belonged to an earlier age, perhaps hundreds of years before Agamemnon was born. Nevertheless, for the second time Schliemann had followed Homer with the blind faith of a true believer and come in a winner.

Schliemann went on. He investigated Crete, where there were reputed to be ruins of palaces even larger than at Mycenae. He dickered with the owner of one such ruin at Knossos on Crete's north coast, and was

Schliemann: He Uncovered a Layer Cake of Troys

HEINRICH SCHLIEMANN: 1822-1890

SOPHIA SCHLIEMANN: 1852-1938

If the events of Heinrich Schliemann's life were set in a novel, the story would be tossed aside as too bizarre to be believed. Born to abject poverty, Schliemann worked as a helper in a tiny general store in rural Germany. But driven by ambition he soon realized that he was locked into a backbreaking routine that would get him nowhere, so he signed on as a ship's boy for a passage to Venezuela. The voyage was just begun when the ship was wrecked and he was cast up, naked and nearly frozen to death, on the shore of Holland. A few years and several jobs later, he was doing important work for a Dutch dealer in commodities. At age 25, Schliemann had a sufficient mastery of the trading business to set up on his own. By the time he was 40—taking big risks, working and scheming around the clock—he had become an international trader with fluency in many languages and a large personal fortune.

A brilliant loner, pathologically shy and suspicious, he filled the barren hours of his life by reading voraciously. In the course of that pursuit he concluded that Homer's *Iliad* was a literal historical document. In 1868 that conviction led him to give up his compulsive drive for yet more wealth and to turn toward Troy.

Having once been married, disastrously, to a Russian—and being uncomfortable with women generally —Schliemann wrote the Archbishop of Athens, who was an old friend, and asked for a favor. He set out the qualifications he thought a good wife should have, and requested that one be found for him. The archbishop came up with a striking-looking 17-year-old Greek village girl, Sophia Engastromenos. Schliemann married her and, surprisingly, the union was a great success. He worshiped Sophia. He trusted her completely, the only human being—other than himself—he did trust. He took her on his archeological trips, and she was with him on June 14, 1873, that broiling day at Troy when he turned up his first pre-Classical gold artifacts.

The site was crawling with workers —each, in Schliemann's eyes, a potential thief. Even though a Turkish overseer was on hand to see that nothing of real value was taken away, Schliemann whispered to Sophia that she should announce it was his birthday and that everybody at the site could take the rest of the day off —with pay—to celebrate. After they left, Schliemann proceeded personally to scrape out a fortune in gold, piece by piece. They wrapped it up in Sophia's big shawl and carried it away.

The prize piece found that day was a diadem of intricately worked chains and bangles. In all, it contained 16,353 pieces of gold. Sophia is wearing it in the photograph at top right.

In his later years after other explorations and discoveries on the Greek mainland, Schliemann built himself a fine house in Athens and filled it with treasures from his various archeological forays. What to do with the gold from Troy remained something of a problem, since the Turkish government was suing to get it back. He finally decided to donate it to the German government and in return managed to wangle the decorations and honors that his fatherland had denied him for so many years. By that time he was a well-known figure in the archeological world. He mellowed, and his wild interpretations of the origins of the gold artifacts were forgiven him in the general recognition of his colossal achievement: the discovery of Mycenaean civilization.

on the point of closing a deal to purchase the site when he thought to count the olive trees, since they were an important part of what he had agreed to buy. Finding that the site contained only 889 trees instead of the 2,500 he was supposed to be getting, he broke off the arrangement in a rage.

After that, Schliemann found no more gold. He did continue his interest in the Bronze Age world, and —though never a professional archeologist—by the time he died in 1890 he had finally begun to comprehend the true nature of the lost world he had stumbled into, something that no one before him had even imagined. When all is said and done, Schliemann must be credited with the discovery of Mycenaean civilization.

Had he been younger, less suspicious, a little less sharp and conniving, Schliemann might have persevered in Crete and found even more spectacular things. As it turned out, success there was reserved for an Englishman named Arthur Evans, who was totally different from Schliemann.

The son of a rich man, Evans found his way into archeology, became the keeper of the Ashmolean Museum at Oxford, traveled extensively in the Balkans and in Greece, searching for antiquities. He became interested in the small carved gemlike seals that were turning up in Greece and on the Aegean Islands in increasing numbers and that could still be bought for ridiculously small sums.

Evans was extremely nearsighted. To examine those seals, which were very small—only an inch or so long—he had to put them close to his eyes. This magnified their detail so much that he was able to appreciate better than others the extraordinary delicacy and originality of their carving. Some seals had hunting scenes on them, some had people, some had ships, some had dolphins. A good many of them appeared to have short inscriptions in an unknown writing that baffled and intrigued him.

He began collecting the seals and quickly realized that some of the most interesting specimens were being found on Crete. He went there in 1894, still more interested in inscriptions than in anything else. But as he became aware of the dimensions of the extensive buried ruin at Knossos, he gradually shifted his interest from carved seals to this larger relic of the past. He decided to excavate it. Endless negotiations followed, complicated by international politics involving Crete's drive for independence from Turkey. Finally, in 1900, the way was cleared and Evans began digging at Knossos. As his half sister, who wrote his biography, later put it, Evans started out by trying to find a seal impression or a clay tablet, and ended up by discovering an entire civilization.

Evans spent the rest of his life and much of a large fortune at Knossos. The ruins there turned out to be an immense palace, with a maze of courtyards, public reception rooms, corridors, private apartments, colonnades, storage vaults, staircases, bathrooms and shrines. Parts of the structure had been several stories high, but were tumbled down by a terrible catastrophe of some kind. It must have been an earthquake, he tentatively decided.

Blackened walls gave evidence of a destructive fire, a fire that had hardened and preserved a great quantity of clay tablets inscribed in the same cryptic writing that had first drawn Evans to Crete when he had detected it on gem seals. Rows of huge clay storage jars, or *pithoi,* stood unbroken in ground-floor storage rooms. Scattered everywhere was an array

Text continued on page 20

Evans: He Discovered a Civilization

When Arthur Evans started work at Knossos in 1900, the site was completely covered with earth and gave almost no hint of the fabulous ruin that lay hidden beneath. In all, it covered about six acres, a low mound rising from a gently sloping hillside.

He began digging with a small local staff, but quickly enlarged it to more than 100 as the size of the palace was revealed. He hired an assistant and a full-time professional architect, one of the first ever on a dig.

Within two years the staff had uncovered the throne room, the main court, the grand staircase and royal apartments—and Evans had made an unprecedented decision: to use steel and concrete members to substitute for missing parts of the palace.

At first Evans' headquarters was a rented villa in nearby Heraklion. After six years of commuting he built his own Villa Ariadne next to the site itself. The digging went on for 35 years—from 1900 to 1935—interrupted each summer because of the intense heat and the threat of malaria. All in all, Evans himself spent about a million dollars on Knossos.

Arthur Evans, in his second season at Knossos, holds a rhyton unearthed in the palace. Before he was finished on Crete more than three decades later, his great finds and masterly analysis of them made him the archeologist of his day, greatly admired for both his iron will and his poet's imagination.

The throne room looked like this in 1901, right after the debris was removed, and before the walls were rebuilt and the frescoes repainted. The throne itself—"Europe's oldest"—is at right. The tent looming in the background held equipment.

These three pithoi, or storage jars, were among the hundreds that Evans found lined up row after row in the palace's lowest level. Some were as much as six feet high. To move them, especially when laden, ropes were attached to the handles.

The grand staircase, Evans' most spectacular architectural discovery—and biggest structural headache—was about half restored when this photograph was taken in 1901. Evans (in white) posed proudly with his second-in-command, Duncan Mackenzie, and with Theodore Fyfe, the first of three architects who helped in the reconstruction of the palace.

*Civilization in the pre-Classical Aegean was an amalgam
of three cultural strands: the Cycladic, the Minoan (on Crete)
and the Helladic (on the Greek mainland). The Early Bronze
Age, a slow period, longer than the Middle and Late combined,
itself saw the blossoming of three distinct Cycladic cultures:
the Grotta-Pelos, Keros-Syros and Phylakopi. After the Third
Millennium B.C., Minoan influence increasingly dominated
the Cyclades until, plagued by earthquake and volcanic
eruption, the Minoans in turn finally succumbed to Mycenaean
culture. The key at right, to the chart opposite, lists the
major episodes in the chronology of the Bronze Age Aegean.*

CHRONOLOGICAL KEY

A. Destruction of Lerna
B. Fall of the first Minoan palaces
C. Eruption of Thera
D. Fall of the second Minoan palaces
E. Fall of the last palace at Knossos
F. Trojan War
G. Fall of the Mycenaean palaces

of smaller pots, beakers, vases and cups, some of clay, some of stone, representing a bewildering variety of art styles. Clearly a people of tremendous vigor and originality—and great wealth—had lived here for a very long time. But who they were or where they came from or—more mysterious yet—what had become of them, he had no idea.

Nor had anyone else. As the years went by, theories multiplied: the Cretans were Egyptians; they were one of the lost tribes of Israel; they were the ancestors of the Phoenicians; of the Greeks. Some thought Crete was the Atlantis of legend, all of whose people had migrated away for some reason (unexplained) to some other place (unidentified), and there vanished (for causes unknown). At the bottom of all this confusion was the awkward fact that Evans, when he started work at Knossos, had no idea of the age or the dimensions of the civilization he was unearthing. But as he began to sort out his enormous haul and to organize its pottery into a proper time sequence, clues began to emerge.

He concluded that the palace at Knossos had been occupied in one form or another for close to a thousand years; that a less elaborate, earlier parent culture had flourished on the same spot for at least another thousand years before that; and that this earlier civilization had its roots in a Late Stone Age culture whose beginnings went back at least another 3,000 years. But what the actual dates were—when this 5,000-year occupancy started and when it ended —Knossos did not say.

Luckily, the Cretans apparently had enjoyed a long trading relationship with Egypt: Egyptian objects have turned up at Knossos and a number of Cretan pots have been recovered from Egypt. Since

Egyptian writing has been deciphered, and since the Egyptians were great ones for carving their names, dates and genealogies on any handy tomb or monument, a fairly precise chronology of Egyptian matters has been known for a long time.

Thanks to that, and the resulting opportunity to cross-check the artifacts traded with Crete, archeologists have succeeded in fitting absolute dates to the later parts of the Cretan sequence. Its flowering and decline covered the aforementioned Bronze Age in the Aegean, a period that began in about 3000 B.C. with the use on the islands of copper and bronze and ended in about 1100 B.C. with the introduction of iron. To this civilization Evans gave the name Minoan, dividing it up into a number of periods and subperiods. The word itself came from the mythical King Minos of Crete.

According to Greek legend, Minos had been given a handsome white bull for sacrifice to the god Poseidon. But Minos thought so highly of the bull that, instead of sacrificing it, he kept it. This enraged the god, who decided to punish Minos by having his wife Pasiphaë fall in love with the bull. She did, and her passion became so obsessive that she persuaded the inventor Daedalus to construct a cowlike model in which she could conceal herself. In that way she satisfied her lust, whose offspring was a monster, a creature with a man's body and a bull's head, known as the Minotaur (the Minos bull). It lived in the dark in a labyrinth underneath Minos' palace at Knossos, feeding on youths and maidens sent as tribute to Minos from the city of Athens.

The legend of the Minotaur goes on to tell how the young Athenian prince Theseus decided to put an end to the payment of tribute. He substituted himself for

EARLY BRONZE AGE		MIDDLE BRONZE AGE	LATE BRONZE AGE
EARLY CYCLADIC		MIDDLE CYCLADIC	Ⓒ
Grotta-Pelos Keros-Syros Phylakopi			
EARLY MINOAN		MIDDLE MINOAN Ⓑ	LATE MINOAN Ⓓ Ⓔ
EARLY HELLADIC Ⓐ		MIDDLE HELLADIC	LATE HELLADIC (MYCENAEAN) Ⓕ Ⓖ

one of the youths bound for Crete and, once there, fell in love with Minos' daughter Ariadne. She gave him a ball of thread to pay out as he entered the labyrinth so he could use it to find his way out again. Theseus killed the Minotaur and escaped with the princess. The story does not end happily for Ariadne, who had sacrificed everything to run off with her lover. On his way back to Athens, Theseus abandoned her on the island of Naxos.

What to make of this tale? Before Evans uncovered Knossos, not much. Now, on the evidence of Minoan art, it has been revealed that bulls were important to Minoan life and sport—and very possibly religion. The labyrinth is pretty obviously a distorted recollection of the size and complexity of the palace at Knossos, where a wide-eyed Greek visitor quickly could have gotten himself lost. The tale of the tribute could reflect a period when Minoan naval power was so dominant in the Aegean that a second-class Mycenaean city like Athens might well have found it prudent to pay tribute, possibly in order to trade on a preferential basis.

Was Minos a real man? No one knows. Most experts believe that the word refers to a title—like Pharaoh—and not to an individual king. If that is so, then there were many Minoses.

Ariadne is more of a problem. It now appears that she represents a goddess of Minoan origin, and the legend of her abandonment on Naxos may be a romantic retelling of the spread of her cult to that island. If that explanation is too vague, myth analyzers can always fall back on a more practical one: Theseus was a hardheaded young man, obsessed with the problems of control and succession at Athens. He may have had a wife there already. If so, it would have been only prudent for him to have dumped this potentially embarrassing Minoan princess on one of the islands he passed on his way home.

However the Theseus myth is interpreted, it is intriguing because it is one of a very few Classical accounts that mention Crete at all—a fact that only increased the astonishment of the archeological world as the extraordinary dimensions of Minoan culture began to emerge. During this century other palaces have been discovered on Crete, together with their surrounding towns. Luxurious country villas have been identified, great numbers of tombs and signs everywhere of smaller settlements, indicating that Bronze Age Crete was densely populated.

While more was being learned about this lost Minoan civilization, so was more being learned about life on the Greek mainland. Sites there were being located and studied constantly, making it clear that what Schliemann had hit upon at Mycenae was only the tip of an archeological iceberg; that a Bronze Age civilization comparable to the Minoan in its richness and its life style flourished there, too, for many centuries. Finally, a third aspect of that same Bronze Age flowering has been detected in the Cyclades, the smaller Aegean Islands that lie scattered across the sea between the Greek mainland and Crete.

It has been the job of archeology to fit all this material together—to relate its three strands to one another, not only in time but in terms of a cultural synthesis that makes sense of the similarities among the three as well as their differences. The job is immense, complicated as it is by other disciplines: linguistics, volcanology, underwater exploration, botanical studies, radiocarbon dating, plus long-range weather studies and the unscrambling of a hitherto indecipherable language—to name a few. All these tools have thrown light on the mystery of Bronze Age Aegean culture, but the light they throw sometimes casts confusing shadows, and even today there are some thunderously large and fundamental questions that have not been answered.

For example, nobody really knows who the people were who would become the Greeks, where they came from or when they arrived. There are all sorts of interesting and plausible theories, just as there are about the origins and fate of the Minoans. The trouble is that a man who studies languages will come up with one scenario, a man who studies volcanoes will come up with another, a man who studies the changes in pottery styles will come up with another, a man who studies Homer and Classical written accounts in an effort to tease out the facts behind the myths will come up with still another. Some day all the evidence being assembled from these various disciplines, with added pieces now lacking, will fit together. It does not fit perfectly at the moment.

In these circumstances it may be that we are posing the wrong question when we ask: "Who were the original Greeks?" Perhaps it does not matter all that much. Perhaps we would be better served if we could find some sort of cultural process that operated in the Aegean, one that could explain the emergence of a civilization without our having to wonder about where the proto-Greeks came from or what kind of cultural baggage they had with them when they arrived. What if a set of conditions could be identified that could produce a civilization without *any* reliance on the migration of peoples?

In short, how does a civilization get started?

Colin Renfrew, a British archeologist specializing in the Bronze Age Aegean, and particularly the Cyclades, asked himself that basic question not long ago when he was pondering some of the perplexities of the Aegean past. Why not assume, he said to himself, that nobody had to come from anywhere, that there were people already living there—as late neolithic remains make very clear—and that they forged a civilization themselves?

This is not the conventional way of looking at the problem. Most scholars adopt a diffusionist view; that is, they seek to explain the rise of a civilization such as the Mycenaean or the Minoan by trying to identify outside influences that triggered it—infiltrators who brought in new ideas or techniques, conquerors who imposed them. Renfrew is an unabashed antidiffusionist. While he acknowledges the existence (and importance) of cross-fertilization through contact between peoples, he does not believe that the contact is all that critical in getting things started. The takeoff from a static subsistence agricultural society can, he theorizes, come from within such a society if the conditions are right.

Before looking at those conditions, it is necessary to understand what a subsistence agricultural society is. It is one in which nobody does much more than he must in order to survive. Its people live in small settlements, widely scattered, relying on simple farming, fishing and the gathering of occasional wild crops such as nuts and fruits for their survival. Within the community there is no social stratification to speak of. That depends on wealth, on display, on inherited privilege, on prowess in war, and since there are no inherited privileges, no wars (other than minor local squabbles over theft of animals or wom-

HOMER'S WHO'S WHO

The Trojan War took place about 1250 B.C. but the poet Homer did not get around to singing about it until some 500 years later. Nevertheless, scholars now agree that Homer's *Iliad* deals with real events, but, because it was handed down through generations of bards, the facts have been pretty badly garbled and romanticized. Thus the story of the Trojan horse, a gift to put the defending Trojans off guard, may or may not have been true. Did the Greek invaders literally build a huge, hollow horse, fill it with warriors and pretend to sail away, counting on the Trojans to open their gates and haul it in as a trophy of victory—and thus ensure their own defeat? Not likely.

The main characters in Homer's epic are, nonetheless, a fascinating group. Their histories are summarized below.

This detail from an Eighth Century B.C. vase, contemporary with Homer, tells the Trojan-horse story. The artist has opened up the side of the horse to make clear that there were Greeks inside.

Agamemnon: King of Mycenae, richest and most powerful of the Greek kings, for that reason chosen to head the expedition to Troy. His greed and pride precipitated a row with Achilles that nearly wrecked the Greek cause. While he was away his wife, Clytemnestra, took a lover, then had Agamemnon murdered when he came home.

Achilles: Leader of an obscure contingent but credited with being the Greeks' best fighter. In a piratical foray en route to Troy, Achilles' share of the booty was a pretty girl named Briseis. But Agamemnon, as the expedition's commander in chief, demanded and got her for himself, infuriating Achilles, who brooded in his tent while the Trojans defeated the Greeks in battle after battle.

Menelaus: King of Sparta and Agamemnon's brother. His wife, the dazzlingly beautiful Helen, ran off with a young Trojan prince, so Menelaus appealed to Agamemnon for help in getting revenge. Agamemnon responded by organizing the expedition to Troy.

Nestor: King of Pylos and probably the second-ranking man on the Greek side. Older than the other commanders, and presumably wiser, he persisted in giving long, windy advice to his fellow warriors.

Ajax: Next to Achilles, the best Greek fighter. Actually, Ajax may have lived earlier, but his exploits were so extraordinary that bards gave him a role in the Trojan story.

Odysseus: King of Ithaca, and the most complex and interesting of the *Iliad*'s heroes. A favorite of the later Classical Greeks because—though not the strongest man around—he triumphed by his wits. Homer's second epic, the *Odyssey,* is about Odysseus' 10-year adventure trying to get home after the fall of Troy. Meanwhile, his wife, Penelope, waited all those years, fending off suitors who wanted to marry her and usurp the throne.

Priam: King of Troy. An old man, unable to fight himself, he sensed that his city was doomed, that he and his sons would die and that his wife Hecuba and all the other Trojan noblewomen would be carried off into slavery.

Hector: Priam's son and Troy's finest warrior. While Achilles sulked in his tent over the loss of Briseis, Hector led the besieged Trojans to victory in a series of skirmishes beneath the city's walls. In one of these actions he killed Achilles' closest friend Patroclus. That brought Achilles out of his sulk. He challenged Hector to single combat and killed him. Then, still possessed by an ungovernable rage, he dragged Hector's corpse by the heels around Patroclus' tomb.

Paris: Also Priam's son, a pretty boy who, in his youth, had been inveigled into judging which of three goddesses was the most beautiful. He chose Aphrodite, who, as a reward, arranged for Paris' seduction of Helen, the world's most beautiful woman, precipitating the Trojan War.

en) and no wealth either beyond the simple possessions needed for survival, social stratification does not occur. There is little or no saving up of things for trade, since trade is virtually nonexistent; everybody for miles around grows and makes the same things. There is little in the way of craft specialization; nearly every person in the community knows how to make, for better or worse, what the others in the community can make. Such a society, once it has worked out a way of surviving comfortably in the environment in which it finds itself, settles firmly into that survival rut. It is extraordinarily resistant to change.

How, then, *does* such a society change? That is Renfrew's question. He is not content with the standard explanation that change is brought about by outsiders. That begs the issue, for it merely passes the question along: Where did the outsiders get *their* culture? Instead, logic demands an agitator of some sort within that static community, something to stir it up, encourage it not only to do things differently, but—more importantly—to keep on doing them differently. If that can happen, then the first twist of an upward spiral of social progress has begun—a spiral that, if it continues, will lead to what could be called a civilization.

The first thing to be remembered, of course, is that no society, no community however small, can exist in a vacuum. Things happen. Better ways of doing things are hit upon. There are cold years and hot ones, droughts, epidemics. Meeting these threats to its equilibrium, a community will alter its habits to the extent that it must. If crops fail, then there will be more fishing, more hunting for wild-food substitutes. If people begin dying from disease, it may be necessary to appease the gods with sacrifices, which

again entails greater expenditure of energy to procure food—enough for the gods, enough for man. But as soon as the emergency is over, the community tends to return to its old ways.

That is the kind of precivilization world that existed in the lands surrounding the Aegean—a static world of small agricultural communities practicing a Stone Age culture. Where the people originally came from is not known. Some had already been there for thousands of years, moving occasionally, changing their life styles slowly in response to the gradual swing toward warmer weather brought on by the easing of the most recent ice age. If there was any diffusion in this world, it is believed to have been the introduction of agriculture and animal husbandry from the Near East, where people had learned to cultivate crops and raise domestic animals some time around 7000 B.C. That practice spread; and since agriculture was superior in some respects to the old way of hunting game and gathering wild foods, it tended to supplant that old way.

People spread with the practice. They came to the Aegean from somewhere to the east: from Anatolia, or from the highlands of Persia, or from around the Black or Caspian seas—no one is sure. What is known is that many of the peoples who were churning about in that vast area for untold generations were related in some way. A number of them are believed to have spoken variations of the same mother language: Indo-European.

But getting back to the question, "Who were the Greeks?" one can say only that they were Indo-Europeans. They, or their ancestors, may have appeared in the Aegean as early as 7000 B.C., mingling with the aboriginal hunters. If that is so, then the language and the people who would later be recognized as Greek evolved right there in Greece.

A contrary view holds that the original Greeks were intruders who appeared from the east shortly before 2000 B.C. In that case, the newcomers probably spoke a language that was proto-Greek.

Whichever view is held, a civilizing process did take place. What was it? How did those people over the millennia come to build towns, fortresses, temples, produce works of art, an elaborate religion and ultimately a written language?

To answer that question Renfrew first asks that the subsistence agricultural settlement of late neolithic times be looked at as a system, a model or pattern whose component parts can be identified. Among those parts—or subsystems—are patterns of family relationships, of land ownership, ways of worship, ways of getting food, ways of making things, ways of socializing and so on. In short, any community, no matter how simple, can be divided into a number of such functions that represent how the people in it conduct their lives.

For a change in living to occur, Renfrew suggests, at least two of the subsystems that make up the community must be affected by the pressure of some trend or influence. If the pressure is not constant—if, for example, it is simply a matter of a seasonal crop failure—the thrust toward change will fade as soon as the emergency is over. But if the pressure is something subtler and more widespread, then other subsystems will be given a nudge. Changes in them will tend to keep the influence going, will reinforce it and in turn will be reinforced themselves. This process of mutual reinforcement is well known to science and has been given the name positive feed-

back. An example for the Aegean would be the development of the olive or the grape, both of which are known to have been introduced into the food subsystems of the region from local wild plants by 3000 B.C., perhaps even earlier.

Grapes certainly played no large part originally in the food subsystem. Grapes were neither very nourishing nor amenable to being stored, as were staple grains like wheat or barley. But they did taste delicious. Furthermore, they grew on steep slopes in the southern Aegean where grain could not easily be grown, providing the community with an alternative potential food supply by utilizing land that previously had little or no value. In addition, it was learned somehow that the juice of grapes could be kept in jugs, where it fermented to make a liquid that tasted different from the fresh juice—and certainly made the drinker feel different.

It is not hard to speculate how these factors, working together, could gradually encourage the devotion of an increasing amount of energy to the cultivation and harvesting of grapes, with unexpected side effects beginning to show up in several other subsystems in the community.

Barter, for example, could have been stimulated among people who didn't have grapes or wine but wished to get them in trade for wheat, fish, pots —whatever extra they could scrape together by greater effort. The grape growers, in turn, often living in steep stony areas, would be encouraged to produce more grapes in order to get the grain that their own land produced so sparingly. Swapping goods leads to the selection of a regular spot where such swapping can take place—to the establishment of a market center—with resultant changes in the

This Minoan wine press, from about 1600 B.C., was found in the service quarters of a villa at Vathypetro in central Crete. Fresh grapes were dumped in the large vat at right and then trodden down by bare feet. Juice from the crushed grapes ran out through a spout into the smaller vessel, next to the vat. The largest pot may have served as a fermenting jar.

physical structure of communities: the creation of public squares, storage areas and so on.

At the social level the warming effects of wine could have had an impact on the habits of the community, encouraging the men to sit around, sipping and talking. Social drinking would have encouraged (and in truth did encourage, according to archeological evidence) an increased emphasis on the making of handsome goblets. That kind of emphasis would have accelerated the beginnings of a division of labor in the community, with craft specialties sorting themselves out according to the aptitudes and interests and opportunities of individual villagers. Pottery as a craft, of course, cannot exist where there is not food to support men who devote all their time to making pots. But when farmers begin to see the advantages of laying aside surpluses to swap for goods, then the potters can be supported.

With craft specialties developing, a further impetus would have been given to swapping and to trade, increasing the importance of the market center. Responsibility for administering this center would have fallen under the control of the strongest, the most just or the most enterprising individuals in the community—probably originally as a matter of orderly barter, but growing to be a mark of prestige, and ultimately exercised as a matter of right.

During this time the intoxicating effects of wine would not have escaped the notice of the villagers. That it made men behave strangely would have endowed wine with a mystical power. Such power would have had religious overtones and might have had a strong effect on the religious subsystem within the community. Something of this sort almost certainly did take place. In later Greek religion there

was a god of wine—or, more properly, of the uncontrolled, emotional side of man that is released by wine: Dionysus. His revels were regularly celebrated by dancing, drinking and sexuality.

One stimulus—the grape: many results. It is in this multiplicity of consequences, in the stimulation of one subsystem by another, that Renfrew finds the ongoing energy, the mutually reinforcing fuel that makes for the retention of changes, and thus provides a climate for further changes. This phenomenon Renfrew calls the multiplier effect. The term is apt because, with change, the opportunity for further change is multiplied—the whole system gathering momentum as it goes.

A scenario similar to that for wine could be written for the olive, and yet another for the introduction of metals, which also made their appearance in Greece and the Aegean around 3000 B.C. Metals, in particular, would have stimulated crafts and trade, and undoubtedly gave a tremendous push to a more subtle process: the evolution of the concept of wealth and the emergence of social classes.

This conclusion needs a little explaining, since in a possession-oriented society such as we have today it is difficult to imagine a community where the concept of wealth does not exist. Conjure up a society where there are little or no savings, where social distinctions based on property are nonexistent because what property a man has is strictly utilitarian. The clay vessels, stone implements, mats and other household things he owns have not been accumulated for their artistic merit, are not regarded as articles of worth but as necessities. A man does not swagger down the street because he is the owner of a clay pot. But when he has a handsomely decorated drink-

ing goblet, perhaps a better one than any of his friends, or if he has saved up to trade for a metal dagger or spear point or even a small ornament to wear, then those things do have value to him, and he begins very gradually to measure his worth by them —and in time to expect others to do the same.

As Renfrew points out, the relationship between material objects and social activities or values is not easy to grasp. Nonetheless, that is where the energy for the interaction of subsystems comes from. The two are related because man, in his activities, related them by putting a social and symbolic value on material goods, thus stimulating a wide range of activities that satisfy his aspirations and needs. At the most primitive level, these activities encourage oversaving, which is a guard against fluctuations in the food supply. In the longer range they provide the emotional and competitive fuel that drives the civ-

ilizing motor. Men want more, they try harder, they stretch their physical and intellectual capacities. And it is those efforts that produce a civilization: that unique human invention whose overall effect is to put a protective shield between man and the hazards of the natural world.

This interpretation does not imply that the civilizing process is a direct cause-and-effect matter. A does not ignite B, which in turn triggers C, and so on. Rather, the process is the result of intricate interplay among a great many elements in a social system, each deriving subtle feedback boosts from others and in turn stimulating them. The example of the stimulative effect of grape cultivation has been offered here in exceedingly simplified form; actually, it is part of a larger and more complex fabric of interwoven forces. Civilizing ferment was undoubtedly bubbling in many other subsystems of the neolithic economy before the grape appeared. Almost certainly there was some social stratification in communities, marked by a growing respect for wealth and thus for the accumulation of possessions among those who already were becoming superior. The possessions were not merely for personal display—to remind the owner and everybody else of his importance—but also for the giving of gifts, those large personal gestures that are so important a part of being a superior person.

Trade, surprisingly enough, also existed in the Aegean long before the appearance of the olive, the grape or metals. There is evidence of it in the distribution of obsidian, a very hard and close-grained volcanic stone much prized for the excellent knives and scrapers that could be made from it. The obsidian trade goes back to 7000 B.C. A remarkable feature of the stone is that its characteristics differ very slightly from place to place; laboratory analysis can determine where a particular piece comes from. The best obsidian in the Aegean was quarried on the island of Melos, and artifacts made of it crop up today in archeological sites on both Crete and the Greek mainland. Clearly, then, obsidian was traded—and it had to be traded for something that others had a surplus of—for pottery, perhaps, or wool.

Whatever the exchange was, it is certain that the feedback process was at first feeble and slow. Until the arrival on the scene of olives, grapes and metals, there wasn't much going on, not much chance to swap things, not much chance to accumulate wealth, to swagger, to bestow fine gifts on visitors. But all three trade materials began to make their presence felt on the Aegean Islands around 3000 B.C. Thereafter the onrush of wealth and culture proceeded at an increasingly rapid rate, and culminated some 1,500 years

later in the brilliant Minoan and Mycenaean palace societies that so astonished the world when Schliemann and Evans began unearthing those unbelievable first bits and pieces of them.

By the time of the palaces, of course, Aegean arts and crafts had become highly developed, and were concentrated under the control of tightly run central bureaucracies. A palace was a combination royal residence, storehouse, religious center, court, social center and accounting office. During the course of its evolution it had gradually grown from a small village bartering center to become a large, rigidly controlled redistribution center.

Note that word redistribution—particularly the "re" at the front of it. When people gathered to barter things it was no longer at their own whim or need but according to the whim or need of a ruler. Part or all of the output of craftsman and farmer—and the payback to them—was regulated and presumably owned by the palace, and redistributed according to strict laws and customs dictated by the palace. These customs—backed up by how much religious sanction we do not know—gradually became old and honored. People accepted them, and their own lowly station in life, without question.

Where did the rulers acquire this control and how was it perpetuated? Presumably it came from the same tendencies that originally encouraged certain men—whether priests, bullies or smooth talkers—to take charge of primitive barter at the village level; perhaps it came from getting buyers and sellers together and providing them with a dependable meeting place for their dickering; perhaps from intimidation. Whatever the means, some of the neolithic settlements that have been studied by archeologists do show—as early as 6000 B.C.—some signs of the existence of a larger chief's house, with evidence of smaller structures clustered closely roundabout. This, if anybody could have recognized it at the time, was the remote ancestor of the palace complex.

As they accumulated goods and a sense of their own importance, chiefs clung to their prerogatives, feeding their pride, looking jealously at neighboring chiefs and probably covetously at their wealth. With valuables worth fighting for hoarded up here and there in village centers, it is reasonably certain that fighting became much more common than it had been in the simpler non-wealth old days.

To hang on to his power a chief had to be an imposing and believable figure at home, a good diplomat abroad and above all a good fighter. So it was inevitable that, as a companion to the development of the concept of wealth, an aristocracy of warriors would emerge. Warriors would owe their allegiance to a super warrior, or king, with relationships intricately worked out through clan affiliations, through blood ties and by the exchange of gifts. The chief dispensed perquisites and favors to his relatives and friends, and rewarded loyalty.

As a result, the concept of entrenched power was slowly established, vested in a ruler and filtered down through him and the members of his family, through a hierarchy of nobles and priests, through military commanders, through regional and local administrators, down to the lowest levels of society. What the lower classes got was an orderly picture of what to expect in life, plus protection in turbulent times.

The final product of this feedback process, unexpected but logical when one thinks about it, is the fortification of towns. This was a group effort that had to be directed by a central authority, that required tremendous labor, careful planning and a commitment over many years. And it became increasingly necessary in a world that was growing more hazardous as a result of the interplay of the feedback forces.

Again, the foregoing is an oversimplification—perhaps a dangerous oversimplification—of a civilizing model that has been worked out in great detail by Colin Renfrew. It is extremely persuasive, and it all hangs together very logically. But is there any truth in it? For that Renfrew bids us look at the civilizations themselves to see what clues they hold that might prove or disprove his theories.

Generally speaking, the model holds up very well. The three cultural threads that emerged in the Aegean —the Cycladic (on the small islands), the Minoan (on Crete) and the Helladic (on the Greek mainland)—appear to have developed largely under their own steam. (The word Helladic derives from the Greek word for Greece: Hellas.) The stages of Helladic culture between the years 1600 and 1100 B.C. are usually referred to as Mycenaean.

All three cultures were enhanced by one another, and from the outside. The potter's wheel and the concept of writing, as examples, were imported—on the evidence that both advances occurred at an earlier time in places other than the Aegean. But such developments are sparks that brighten a fire that has already been ignited. Enterprising Cycladic potters simply incorporated the new technique of the wheel and made better Cycladic-style pots, and so on.

What about the theory that the grape and the olive were critical in sending the Aegean civilizing process into orbit? An ingenious way of testing this question would be to count the number of settlements that were established in various parts of the Aegean world during the time that these two new crops were making their impact felt—on the proposition that a rising cultural level should be (and, in fact, usually is) accompanied by a significant rise in population.

Here a surprising fact surfaces. Admitting the difficulties encountered in trying at this late date to identify *all* the little settlements that existed in the Aegean some five or six thousand years ago, it is still possible to get a pretty good idea of population distribution and growth by counting—and then comparing—the numbers of communities that *have* been identified in various parts of that world. When this is done, a very suggestive pattern indeed emerges.

In northern Greece, where the principal agricultural products were wheat and barley harvested from extensive flatlands, the growth in the number of settlements was only about 50 per cent during a 1,500-year period between 4000 B.C. and 2500 B.C. By contrast, in the southern part of the Aegean world —in the Cycladic islands, in the southwest Peloponnesus and on Crete—the number of settlements more than quintupled during that same period.

A dry statistic but meaningful. Obviously there was much more going on in the south, where grape and olive grew, than there was up north, where their cultivation was difficult. The southern country was steep and broken up: a varied terrain that encouraged a mixed agricultural economy. And the climate was right. As a result, grape and olive became enormously important in the economies of the southern Aegean, and the area forged ahead. Archeological sites bear this out: storage jars galore for oil and wine, drinking cups, olive oil presses and much evidence

of both grape and olive recorded in the local art that has been uncovered.

The influence of that third civilizing energizer —metals—can also be detected through archeology. Metals sparked a great upsurge in trade and wealth. This fact is made plain by the rapid increase in number, richness and variety of the burial objects found in graves. All in all, the Third Millennium B.C. in the Aegean—about which little was known until recently and which was long thought by scholars to have been backward and barbaric—is now emerging as neither. It was, in fact, an extraordinarily lively period. And of the three strands that make up Aegean culture, the Cycladic in the early days may well have been the liveliest.

The reason for this remains obscure. It may have been location: easy access to the other islands, to the Greek mainland, to Anatolia. It may have been that the islands of the Cyclades themselves were small; on a little island the emergence of a single town as the dominant element could have taken place more rapidly than might have been the case on the mainland or on a big island like Crete where political struggles necessarily would have been on a larger scale and potentially more complex (and perhaps more savage). Early centralization of authority would have resulted in the early creation of a central redistributive system, the earlier development of a controlling hierarchy, a more rapid evolution of craft specialization and more trade.

For these reasons the Cyclades should be looked at first—not only to see what their particular brand of Bronze Age civilization was like, but also to test the Renfrew model: Could that civilization have developed for the reasons he suggests?

Aegean Pottery—the Story It Tells

Only a professional archeologist can truly appreciate the pivotal importance of pottery in unraveling prehistoric events and cultures. Throughout the ancient Mediterranean world good clay was abundant and techniques were developed early for firing it in kilns to make containers. As fast as the pots were damaged or broken, they were thrown out. But the smashed bits—or shards—were as hard as rock and accumulated rapidly under earth floors or on town rubbish heaps. As a result, every ancient archeological site contains masses of them.

When a site is excavated, shards are collected and a careful record is made of the different levels at which they are found. This done, an expert can reconstruct a cultural sequence for a given place by noting the changes in shape and in ornamentation as the site is worked more deeply and thus backward in time. Also, whole pots can sometimes be reconstructed from broken bits.

This technique has enabled archeologists to sort out the various stages of cultural development in the Aegean, where all the pottery sequences can be fitted together with some precision, revealing not only what was going on culturally in various places, but the order in which events happened. The illustrations on the following pages trace that story by showing selected pots unearthed on Crete, the Cyclades and mainland Greece. (The paintings are based on originals in museums; dimensions are for height unless otherwise indicated.)

Shaped like a modern shopping bag, this pottery container, dating from about 1500 B.C., is decorated with a repetitive double-ax design, a major motif in Minoan culture. The artifact, eight inches high, probably was inspired by a prototype made of leather.

Early Bronze Age: 3000-2000 B.C.

EARLY CYCLADIC

In its first stages, Early Cycladic pottery was characterized by incised triangular or herringbone patterns (first two pots, right). Later, circular or spiral designs were popular (third and fourth pots). Painted work dominated the end of the period as dark geometric patterns were added to lighter backgrounds (last two pots). The pyxis, or small lidded jar—of which three examples are shown—was very common but its use is uncertain. The fourth container, viewed from its decorated bottom side, is a so-called frying pan. No one knows its function. One imaginative suggestion: it may have been filled with water and used by Cycladic ladies as a mirror.

Pyxis (4½ inches)

Jar (7½ inches)

EARLY MINOAN

Early Minoan potters played down incised patterns in favor of colorful glazes. Sometimes they used a pattern of faint lines (first piece) to make a ceramic goblet look like a wooden one. The second pot reflects an Early Minoan trend: emphatic dark patterns on lighter backgrounds. The third and fourth pots, examples of mottled ware, are also unmistakably Minoan, featuring blotches of color. The last two objects are rhytons: ritual vessels. Liquids were usually poured in through the rhyton's head. But openings for decanting depended on the vessel: the bull was drained as the fluid poured from its mouth; in the last figure it gushed from the breasts.

Goblet (8½ inches)

Pitcher (11 inches)

EARLY HELLADIC

Unlike the Early Cycladic and Early Minoan styles, the oldest of the Early Helladic pottery was undecorated. Instead the mainlanders developed Urfirnis ware, produced by coating their pieces with a very fine liquid clay slip. When baked, the result was a glossy surface that often gleamed like metal. The first four objects at right have this Urfirnis finish. Toward the end of the Early Helladic period painted designs became increasingly common (last two objects). Nearly all Early Bronze Age pottery was shaped by hand; the potter's wheel, although already well known throughout the Near East, had not yet been widely introduced in the Aegean.

Amphora (17¾ inches)

Amphora (26 inches)

Pyxis (2¾ inches)

"Frying pan" (8¼ inches, diameter)

Sauceboat (6 inches)

Pyxis (2 inches)

"Teapot" (5½ inches)

Pitcher (13 inches)

Rhyton (8 inches)

Rhyton (7 inches)

Sauceboat (4 inches)

Pitcher (8½ inches)

Tankard (8 inches)

Cup (4½ inches)

Middle Bronze Age: 2000-1500 B.C.

MIDDLE CYCLADIC

After 2000 B.C. Cycladic wares became a mixture of older island traditions and introduced Minoan styles as the influence of Crete spread through the islands. The earliest Minoan impact was reflected in a much greater emphasis on painted rather than incised patterns, even while the traditional island motifs were continued (first three pieces at right). Thereafter, and particularly on the island of Thera (last three pots), the vibrant, polychromatic Minoan approach dominated all the islands' ceramic designs, though local potters felt free to create shapes of their own. An outstanding example of that independence is the oblong dish, a form found only on Thera.

Jar (10¾ inches)

Plate (9 inches, diameter)

MIDDLE MINOAN

By the Middle Bronze Age the potter's wheel was in general use in the Aegean, encouraging more daring and elaborate shapes. Minoan craftsmen began producing great quantities of lavishly decorated Kamares ware (first four pieces at right), characterized by two- or three-color designs on a dark background. The cup is an example of eggshell ware, very thin and delicate. The pitcher features the stylized floral pattern that would be eclipsed toward the end of the period by the starfish, shells and seaweed of the mature Marine style shown in the graceful vessel at far right. A rhyton, it belongs to a later date but continues Middle Minoan decorative traditions.

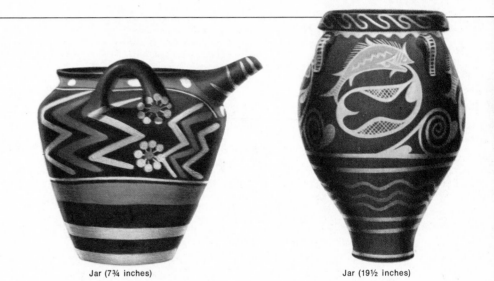

Jar (7¾ inches)

Jar (19½ inches)

MIDDLE HELLADIC

Minyan ware was the common product of mainland Greece at the beginning of the Middle Bronze Age. Created to resemble more valuable metal vessels, it has a slick-looking slip finish that is usually gray (first piece at right) but sometimes black (second piece) or yellow, depending on the kind of raw clay used. Helladic taste, ever conservative, next turned to mat-painted vessels (last four pieces), which are less dashing than the much more ebullient Cycladic and Minoan motifs. The two-handled cups are typical of the Helladic design traditions in the Middle Bronze Age and are among the few new shapes that were introduced by potters working on the mainland.

Goblet (7½ inches)

Cup (4 inches)

Pitcher (12 inches)

Dish (18 inches, length)

Strainer (8½ inches)

Tripod (11½ inches)

"Fruit stand" (21¼ inches, diameter)

Cup (4¾ inches, diameter)

Pitcher (10 inches)

Rhyton (13 inches)

Jar (35 inches)

Amphora (9¾ inches)

Cup (4 inches)

Jar (12¼ inches)

Late Bronze Age: 1500-1100 B.C.

LATE CYCLADIC

After the collapse of the palaces on Crete about 1450 B.C., Minoan influence on Cycladic pottery—which had been a dominant feature throughout the Middle Bronze Age—waned, and the potters of the smaller islands found themselves exposed to a second powerful stylistic onslaught: the Mycenaean. Throughout the Late Bronze Age, aggressive Mycenaean traders pushed their wares all through the Aegean. Against this competition Cycladic potters did continue to produce, but they began to lose their own sense of artistic identity. In the process the pottery of the islands vanished as a distinct style; there is no Late Cycladic pottery sequence.

LATE MINOAN

When the great palace at Knossos was occupied by the Mycenaean invaders, the pottery on Crete underwent an abrupt change, as if the Mycenaeans had put a heavy thumb on the rollicking Marine style (previous page) and imposed their own predilections. The result was the so-called Palace style (first three pieces at right). Fine works all, they nevertheless exude a formality and pomposity that may reflect the character of Mycenaean society itself. With the passage of time the efforts of Minoan potters deteriorated further. Though their work could still be boldly conceived, execution became heavily stylized, with details often sketchy (last three pieces).

Jar (27 inches)　　　Pitcher (19½ inches)　　　Jar (38 inches)

MYCENAEAN (LATE HELLADIC)

Unburdened by outside influences, Mycenaean pottery of the Late Bronze Age is generally of excellent craftsmanship and freer and more fantastic in concept than the Minoan pieces of this period. For the first time, pots of a popular shape and design were made in large volume to meet the demands of the marketplace. An important Mycenaean ceramic contribution was the introduction of the human figure as a major element in their designs. Another innovation was the narrow-stemmed drinking goblet (third piece at right). Marine motifs were always in favor: Argonauts (first piece), cuttlefish (third piece) and octopuses (fourth and sixth pieces).

Jar (21¼ inches)

Vessel (14½ inches)

Although the uses to which the Aegean peoples put their pottery are often obvious—cups for drinking, pitchers for pouring, large jars for storage—the purpose of some of the items often defies explanation and leaves a tantalizing blank in the archeologists' jigsaw.

Was the oblong container on page 35 meant to serve fish? Was the platter just below it for fruit? No one knows. And the little pyxis, or lidded jar, so widely used during the Early Cycladic period, was designed to hold something—but what? If this overwhelmingly common object was intended for trinkets (glass beads, metal pins, jewels), it would mean that Cycladic women went in heavily for personal ornaments. But if it *was* a jewel box, why did its popularity end during a later period, when Cycladic women presumably indulged in *more* self-ornamentation? The so-called frying pan on page 33 was definitely not a cooking utensil; if it were, its underside would not have been decorated. Equally puzzling is the cup with three spouts next to the frying pan. Was it a ritual vessel passed from hand to hand, each drinker using his own spout?

The speculative process that emerges from questions like these shows the enormous distance scholarship has yet to go in solving the everyday riddles posed when archeologists dig into the past. It emphasizes why detailed site development has become so important: where a particular piece is found, the things that accompany it, the frequency with which it recurs can be as significant as the shape of the piece itself.

Jug (11¼ inches)

Vessel (9½ inches)

Pyxis (6 inches)

Goblet (7½ inches)

Filler (14¾ inches)

Vase (14 inches)

Jar (10¼ inches)

Chapter Two: The Bronze Age Cyclades

Sprinkled southeast across the Aegean from the tip of the Attica peninsula is a spatter of little islands. These are the Cyclades, the peaks of ancient mountains poking out of the sea. From 30,000 feet in the air in an intercontinental jet they look like brown leaves floating on a bright-blue plate. The largest of them is about 20 miles long, the size of the Massachusetts island of Martha's Vineyard. From there they range downward to modest humps not more than four or five miles across. Midway in the size range is Melos, 12 miles long and containing about 5,000 people. Over the centuries its population has fluctuated with the fortunes of the Aegean generally, but never very widely. It could well have approached 5,000 when the celebrated Athenian historian Thucydides was a boy.

Thucydides lived about 2,400 years ago, which puts him considerably nearer to us in time than to the people who first settled on Melos—a rather mind-bending thought when one remembers that Thucydides is generally considered an "ancient Greek."

He was an Athenian aristocrat and military leader who fought in the Peloponnesian War, the long struggle between Athens and Sparta. After losing a battle, he was retired from his command and devoted the rest of his career to writing a history of the war. In it he described the crushing of Melos in 416 B.C. by the Athenians. He also speculated with great intelligence

The head at left, from Amorgos island, is characteristic of the enigmatic figurines that were the unique contribution of Early Bronze Age sculptors in the Cyclades. This piece, which measures 14 inches high, is all that has been recovered of a full figure that must have been nearly as big as life. It is a particularly remarkable find, since most of the hundreds of figurines from the islands are less than one third that size.

about the origins of all Greeks. But his speculations fell far short of the truth. Nothing in his mind, or in the mind of any man of his day, could have permitted the bold idea that the ancestors of the Melians he knew might already have been living on their island for nearly 4,000 years.

There is no nailing down that first settlement date precisely. People were going to Melos for obsidian as early as 7000 B.C., but that knowledge is based on the finding of Melian obsidian in other places. On Melos itself—in fact, throughout the Cyclades—the oldest evidence of human occupancy dates from about 4000 B.C. People may have settled there earlier; it is logical that they should have, on the grounds that it is hard to picture 3,000 years of visiting without anyone's having decided to stay. But solid archeological evience for that has not yet been turned up by scholars.

A tough question surfaces here: From which direction did those first settlers come? From the west (the Greek mainland) or from the east (Asia Minor)? The west would seem to be the most reasonable answer. Standing on lofty Cape Sounion a few miles below Athens, one can look southward at a chain of islands stretching away across the water. On clear sparkling days they stand out sharply and seem remarkably close. To a late neolithic coastal dweller of the Greek mainland, they surely must have beckoned. Although early mariners were reluctant to set forth to destinations they could not see—preferring, rather, to hug the shore in the small primitive boats they used—they did travel widely. A jump across to the nearest of the Cyclades—a mere 13 miles away —would have seemed like nothing. A boatful of men certainly could have rowed across in half a day.

Stone mortars, like the one above, were used by Bronze Age Cycladic sculptors to grind colors, which were then kept in cockleshells (right). The purpose of the pigments was to tint marble figurines, which—like the later statues of Classical Greece—were, by custom, brightly painted to indicate facial features, necklaces, skin color and even possibly tattoos. This practice is confirmed by traces of red and blue still adhering to some Cycladic figurines.

From that nearest Cycladic island, Kea, more islands spread out in all directions. Whenever settlement may have started on any of them, it is pretty certain to have followed in short order on the others. Out of these successive settlements, what is known as Cycladic culture emerged.

In its beginnings, of course, the culture of the Cyclades was identical with the Stone Age mainland culture from which it sprang. But on the islands it began to go its own way. At what point it became identifiable as Cycladic is not easy to say, nor is it easy to determine when it ceased to be an emerging subsistence economy and could be labeled a civilization. Such evolutionary boundaries are very fuzzy; after all, one does not find an ape in one generation and a man in the next. If one slices through a Cycladic archeological site at an arbitrary date in time —2500 B.C., say—does one encounter a civilization? Put that way, the question cannot be answered flatly.

Clearly, the palace societies that reached their peak on Crete a thousand years later can be identified as "civilization"; they had the three minimum ingredients that many scholars insist are necessary: (1) large size, towns of at least 5,000 people; (2) a written language; (3) a state religion with monumental religious centers or palaces.

The Cyclades during the Early Bronze Age lacked these criteria. They had no written language, no monumental religious centers or palaces, and their towns were probably a good deal smaller than the 5,000 minimum cited. Nevertheless, it is unfair to call them uncivilized. They need a better, more flexible definition of civilization, and Colin Renfrew has suggested one: "The gradual creation by man of a larger and more complex environment, not only in the natural field through increasing exploitation of a wider range of resources, but also in the social and spiritual fields." This definition was formulated by Renfrew to distinguish between the Cycladic culture of the Early Bronze Age and the Minoan culture that flowered on Crete during the Middle Bronze Age—with a dividing date at about 1700 B.C. But it is still useful for describing the actual developmental process that was taking place in the Cyclades—particularly if one bears down hard on the word gradual.

Gradual it was. The process gathered momentum over a period of more than a thousand years; but even in its earliest-known phases, it gave off sparks of a civilization emerging, with all the murkiness and shapelessness of outline that are associated with very slow progress.

Recent scholarship divides Cycladic culture into three distinct phases. The first is known as Grotta-Pelos, deriving its name from two sites—one on Naxos and one on Melos—that have been worked by archeologists. Grotta-Pelos, extending in time from about 3100 B.C. to about 2600 B.C., stands at the very threshold of the Bronze Age. It can be regarded as a sort of doorway between the old world of the Stone Age Aegean and the new world of metals, expanding trade and advancing civilization.

Grotta-Pelos settlements have been detected on many of the Cyclades. They were small and were usually located close to the shore. Already the people of this culture had abandoned the older neolithic practice of burying their dead under the floors of their houses or in the narrow alleys between. Instead they used cemeteries, usually choosing sites farther inland, often on a slope of ground behind the village. They began to take increasing pains with their burials, making graves from stone slabs set in the ground to form tomblike cavities around the corpses. These so-called cist graves do not show above the surface of the earth. For archeologists the practice has proved to be a boon. Thanks to that stone facing, Grotta-Pelos graves are as durable as they are unobtrusive.

Thanks to the tremendously long time that the culture endured, they are extremely numerous. Thanks, finally, to the dearth of metal objects among the grave materials that were buried with the dead, a large number of graves survived unplundered right into the 20th Century.

Unfortunately that long security has in modern times been shattered. A rage to collect Grotta-Pelos pottery, and particularly the exquisite stone figurines that characterize Cycladic culture, has led to a great speculative boom in their value and to a ruthless rifling of Grotta-Pelos cemeteries. As a result, a chance for valuable site analysis by professionals is gone forever in many places, as are also gone a large number of skeletons whose assembly and study would have provided a priceless scientific picture of the variations in size and shape of those long-lost people—a picture of an entire population.

For all this, a good deal of Grotta-Pelos material has survived. The most characteristic container used by the culture is a rather heavily made pottery bowl with a thick rolled rim that turns in slightly around the lip. Bowls of this type are dark in color and burnished on the surface—that is, the clay was smoothed by being rubbed with a pebble or other instrument, not only for a more attractive appearance but also to help seal the bowl's porosity before firing. A bewildering variety of pottery styles sprang up and died during the Aegean Bronze Age. It is worth pausing over the Grotta-Pelos styles, and some of the others illustrated on pages 31-37, if only to take in the enormous importance of pottery in interpreting the cultural sequences of the past.

In addition to pots, Grotta-Pelos graves yield necklaces of beads made from local stones, together with stone containers of various shapes that again follow an Aegean rather than a Near Eastern or an Egyptian style. These containers are almost always made of marble, occasionally with human limbs and breasts carved in relief on their outer surfaces.

Obviously, a marble drinking cup was infinitely more difficult to make than a clay one and was therefore of much greater value. That fact breathes only one of the many messages that can be heard whispering from the Grotta-Pelos graves: men who could afford marble drinking cups prized them; when they died their high station in the community was acknowledged and these valuable possessions were buried with them; lesser men were interred with lesser objects. So it is clear that there was a stratified society already in the process of establishment among the Grotta-Pelos people, a highly developed religion, wealth beginning to accumulate and a division of labor (indicated by progress in the arts and crafts). Here, plainly revealed by these simple graves, are the forces that would lead to the splendid palace societies of the next millennium.

The grape and the olive flourished during Grotta-Pelos, but of the third cultural energizer—metals —there is scarcely any evidence. Smelting was just making its way into the Stone Age world; in 3000 B.C. its techniques had scarcely penetrated the Aegean. In due course smelting would take hold as recoverable deposits of copper, lead, silver and arsenic were gradually located on the islands and on the mainland.

Not all ores are pure. The earliest metalsmiths, naturally enough, did not recognize this. They often found themselves working with various metallic compounds of whose true nature they were not sure. All

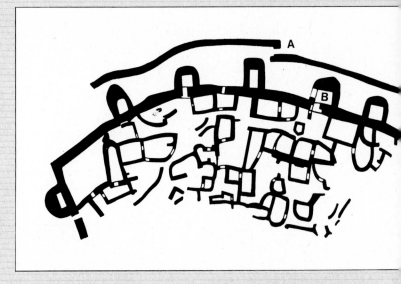

This ground plan points up the features of a citadel that once stood at Chalandriani, on the island of Syros. Such fortifications began appearing in the Cyclades after 2500 B.C. as protection against pirates. The citadel stood on a steep hill, facing the sea and guarding the settlement below. Its main wall (heaviest line) included six rounded parapets, where defenders could stand and slash at attackers as they breeched the smaller outer wall or squeezed through the one opening in it (A). The main entrance (B) was so narrow that only one man at a time could pass through. The irregular shapes inside the fortress are the foundations of houses.

they could tell was that a particular ore from one place worked better than the ore mined at another.

The best copper ore, for example, contained traces of arsenic and produced a much harder and more valuable metal than pure copper did, although the early smith did not know why. The best he could do was seek out this "better" copper and use it. Unfortunately, the arsenic in it was deadly poisonous; the smelting process must have caused an extremely high death rate among metalworkers. This danger may have led to progress in metallurgy through efforts to find less lethal substitutes by mixing copper with silver and even with lead. But those attempts were failures: the resulting compounds were either too brittle or too soft to be useful. The Bronze Age did not really get underway until it was discovered that the best alloy of all was produced by a mixture of copper and tin.

Copper was abundant on the island of Cyprus to the east and in many other places in and around the Aegean, but tin was probably extremely scarce. Small quantities of it were produced in the Near East, but where the bulk of it came from remains a mystery. There has been speculation that the Minoans and Mycenaean Greeks may have traveled west to exploit deposits in Spain and Britain, but there is no proof that they did.

By 2500 B.C. metals were moving freely through the Aegean. The Grotta-Pelos culture faded and was replaced by another, which ran from about 2600 to 2300 B.C. Named Keros-Syros for two Cycladic islands, it is distinguished from its predecessor by a greatly expanded use of metals, accompanied by an overall splurge of affluence. Grotta-Pelos, looked at today,

has a certain starveling, minimal quality about it. Keros-Syros has a sense of abundance.

Villages get bigger, with indications that there was some kind of administrative control in those growing communities, organized around the cental distribution of goods. Graves become more elaborate, their contents more varied and sophisticated. New forms of pottery appear: the one-handled cup and the sauceboat (a container with a handle on one side and a spout on the other—in short, an embryo pitcher). For the first time also, graves and living sites begin to contain significant numbers of metal objects: spear points, daggers and a wide variety of ornaments. A fortress ruin at Chalandriani on the island of Syros has yielded a lovely silver diadem with a design of stars, animals and birds pricked in its surface.

If there is any doubt about the role played by metals as a stimulator of trade and of an upwardly bounding culture, Keros-Syros should dispel it. Not only is there evidence of a clear increase in wealth and display, but there is also a sense of outreach. Grotta-Pelos was parochial; Keros-Syros was not. Its style extends throughout the Aegean and touches mainland Greece, Crete and Anatolia. Here, quite clearly, was a world of active trade with the Cycladic islands strategically placed near the center of it, getting and giving in all directions.

The price of this progress—and fulfilling the claim of Professor Renfrew's model—was greater competitiveness and more fighting. At the older subsistence-settlement level, fights were almost certainly short, precipitated by local theft or insult, and probably never involving more than two adjacent communities. The weapons used by villagers included slings (on the evidence of numerous pellets, both stone and clay, found in early sites) and spears (on the evidence of metal spear tips).

New metal weapons gave a new and more dangerous flavor to Keros-Syros society. The dagger made its appearance. It would soon grow into a terrible agent of destruction—the bronze sword—and the warrior would be born. Now men could go on deliberate forays with the hope of finding valuable loot in neighboring settlements. The target towns had to defend themselves, and they did it with fortifications.

The stronghold of Chalandriani on the island of Syros is a fine example. Remains of a stout wall, with six semicircular bastions sticking out from it at intervals to aid in defense, can still be seen there. Clearly there were local dynasts at work now, able to organize the labor of others and to offer security in return for it. Inside the defensive wall are the foundations of a jumble of small buildings, indicating that the citadel, though only about 50 yards across, was lived in—perhaps used as the headquarters of the chief—and could offer protection to the other members of the small surrounding community whenever threatened by a raid.

The appearance of fortifications on a significant scale in the Keros-Syros culture attests to the growing threat of such raids, as does the beginning—after about 2000 B.C.—of a decline in the number of settlement sites in the Cyclades. Again, the early peaking of Cycladic culture (vis-à-vis that on Crete or mainland Greece) may have been connected in some way with the rather rapid consolidation of control on each of these smaller islands under a central fortress-settlement. It seems logical that this process would have been accelerated by the growth of wealth and by its handmaiden: piracy. Piracy does not flour-

Animal-shaped vessels were common in the Bronze Age Aegean. Less than five inches high, this piece, from the island of Syros, is apparently a bear or hedgehog. Its features are delineated in lustrous black paint on natural clay. The bowl in the animal's paws may have been used to hold honey.

ish without wealth; it is an outgrowth of trade, of familiarity with the sea, of the building of better ships and of greed. It forces the development of fewer, stronger places and gives those places the muscle to venture forth on piratical forays.

At this enormous remove in time—with no names, no accounts, no personalities, no events, no smallest shred of actual written history, not even the ghost of a myth—it is difficult to more than guess at what went on among those Cycladic communities. Was each island its own fortress, with every other island regarded as potential prey or predator, depending on its power? Or were there alliances? Were the island barons dedicated to piracy as a way of life among themselves, thereby accelerating their own fortress evolution? Or can the islands be regarded as simple trading communities trying to get along together in peace, trying to survive onslaughts from other people farther away?

The latter idea can be characterized, in a sense, as diffusionist. But it seems more reasonable to assume that piracy, like the islands' other cultural advances (and in this context piracy must be accepted as a kind of advance), was indigenous to the islands. On this point, however, the archeology of the Aegean tells us nothing for certain. All it can do is continue to trace the general outline of Cycladic development.

Keros-Syros, in its turn, went into decline and was supplanted by the Phylakopi culture, a name drawn from a town on the island of Melos. Its dates are roughly 2300 B.C. to 2000 B.C.

Though the three Cycladic cultural phases are distinct, with clear differences in their pottery and other cultural attributes, it should be emphasied that they still represent a continuum. Some new things are introduced; many others simply continue. For example, the beaked pouring vessels and other pottery objects found at Phylakopi are clearly related to earlier forms that are found in Keros-Syros; they follow a trend and develop from it.

Were the new objects or developed trends the result of outside stimulation brought in by traders? Did they reflect changing fashions at home or the work of local innovators? Did they mark the passing through (even perhaps the settling in) of strangers? Who now can say? Whatever the stimulating source, Phylakopi is noteworthy for two things: it introduced the rock-cut tomb to the Cyclades and produced the only Third Millennium Cycladic settlement, so far known to archeologists, that is large enough to be called a true town. Phylakopi lay strung along the edge of a cliff overlooking the sea. In its heyday its population may have been in the thousands. Why did it not go on to become an even richer and more elaborate place and emerge as a true palace center?

A fascinating and tantalizing question. At the heart of it is the matter of island size. After about 2200 B.C., probably as a consequence of piracy, the number of Cycladic settlements shrank. The smallest ones disappeared; those that survived became bigger and better fortified. Some moved farther inland. All these trends bespeak piracy. A place like Phylakopi was clearly a survivor—and possibly a cannibal—emerging as the biggest and strongest in its immediate neighborhood. But Phylakopi was located on a small island with a limited amount of arable land. Beyond a certain point it could not grow. Its arts and crafts, along with its local resources, at some point reached a limit of exploitability within the technological and social framework of the culture in which it existed. To become more elaborate it would have had to find a broader base to support that elaborateness.

There may be a rule here: other things being equal, the ultimate level to which a culture can aspire is determined by the size and richness of the area—more specifically, the size of the redistributive system—in which the culture operates.

The Aegean appears to be a neat example of the rule at work. Cycladic culture—flowering on small islands, with island-sized redistributive systems—could go just so far. In other places, where the climate and living conditions were similar but the places themselves much larger—in Crete and southern Greece—the process did not stop. In fact, what finally happened to Phylakopi is that a burgeoning Crete reached out and swallowed it. Not literally; there is no archeological evidence for or against a physical Minoan conquest of that old Cycladic town. The takeover was cultural—an artistic and symbolic one. The lively and distinctive pottery styles of Phylakopi were increasingly invaded by Minoan influences. After about 1700 B.C. those indigenous styles were, to all intents, obliterated. The Cyclades became cultural backwaters, leaving the continuing story of Aegean civilization to be told by the archeology of the Minoans and the Mycenaeans.

But during that period of more than a thousand years —the so-called Early Bronze Age—what a lively little world the Cyclades was. Traveling among the islands today in one of the little steamers that stop at even the smallest of them, one can still get some sense of what life must have been like there 4,000 or more years ago. One sees the same blue sea, the same up-thrusting mountain peaks—the most obvious difference being that the slopes are mostly raw and eroded now, their vegetation limited to coarse bushy stuff. Formerly many were forest-clad, and the soil was rich and productive.

The climate is gorgeous. Sometimes there is a sea-softness to the air that blurs the horizon. Sometimes it is as clear and as sharp as a knife. Breezes blow most of the time. Only in the little folded inland valleys does it become stifling in the dog days. Occasionally there are storms. In summer they usually hit from the north—high winds that blow for days and keep the fishing boats ashore. In winter the gales normally strike from the south, whining over the mountain ridges; and while it is never bitterly cold—no frost or snow except near the tops of the higher mountains—what chill there is can penetrate to the bone. The stone walls of the houses exude cold and damp as surely as they have done since the first stone house was built on the islands.

Cycladic houses were small, and the rooms in them even smaller, often not more than six feet long, with space in them for a cot or two and not much else. Wall surfaces of the early period were not finished off. Later ones, as in the island houses today, were covered with plaster and often painted. Modern villages in the Cyclades gleam with whitewash. No wood at all is used except for doors, sills and window frames; there is none to spare. Formerly there was plenty, and it may well have been used in the superstructure of buildings—wooden or clay-brick upper stories on stone foundations—and was almost certainly used for making ceiling beams. Houses were probably cozier in winter too, because of the ready availability of firewood.

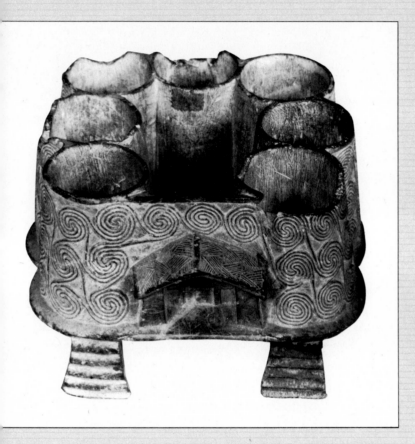

The six-inch-high object above, made of stone and found at Melos, is believed to be a model of an aboveground Cycladic granary. It was divided into several compartments so that different materials could be stored at the same time. The legs served to keep the granary off the ground, out of the wet and away from rats, ever problems in an agricultural society.

Daily life revolved around fishing and trading with neighbors, both on nearby islands and the Greek mainland, with which the Cyclades maintained close and seemingly frequent relationships. People on the land occupied themselves with small farming, olive and grape culture, the tending of flocks of goats and sheep, woodcutting, weaving and such specialized crafts as pottery and metalwork.

The islanders were not only middlemen in a trading world but also exporters of their own goods. There were metal deposits on some of the Cyclades. Each island produced its own local wine. Two—Naxos and Paros—were famous for the quality of their marble. As a result, the islanders had what today would be called a favorable balance of trade, and they became prosperous. By the middle of the Third Millennium B.C., the principal towns on the larger islands had probably grown to a point where they could sustain a full range of activities, and the even tenor of life proceeded on its seasonal round, interrupted only by war and piracy.

When a raid came, and if the settlement was well fortified with a good supply of food and water within the walls, the inhabitants, caught by surprise, crowded into the citadel. They watched with as good a countenance as they could the burning and looting of their homes, the wasting of their fields and the carting off of their livestock and boats. As they waited for the raiders to go away, they were already planning how and when they would mount a reprisal raid of their own a year or two later.

Again, there is no way of knowing what kinds of local alliances were forged among the small Bronze Age island kingdoms. It may be that a paramount chief from time to time managed to gather several islands under his control for purposes of larger raids on others, or perhaps for more ambitious and more peaceful trading expeditions to far places. What is certain is that there was a great deal of movement among the islanders. Despite fights, the people knew one another well and mixed freely. Culturally they lived in one world—a world of dawning wealth, of dawning display, of dawning social and political aspirations. Manpower was the principal energy source. The windmills that in later centuries would line the island ridges like rows of sentinels were as yet unknown. If grain was to be ground, it was done by hand in a primitive stone grinder—a quern. If a load had to be hauled, it was moved by men or perhaps by oxen; there were no horses. Considering the amount of stone that was quarried, trimmed and wrestled into place to form even the simple fortifications of the Cyclades, the man-hours involved were certainly formidable.

The spiritual side of a Cycladic islander is difficult to assess. Basically he was a pragmatist, getting his livelihood from a fairly rough environment, respectful of the wealth and power that was beginning to creep into his society, suspicious of strangers, suspicious of change. But, to balance that suspicion, he was enterprising to a remarkable degree, and had a view of the world that was surely broadened by his position in it: he was standing at the crossroads of all the cultural influences and political forces that were passing through.

Still, he was much more than a pragmatist. The late German philosopher Ernst Cassirer, in his *An Essay on Man,* has written: "Man lives in a symbolic universe [of which] language, myth, art and religion are parts. They are the varied threads which weave the . . . tangled web of human experience. . . . Physical reality seems to recede in proportion as man's symbolic activity advances. Instead of dealing with the things themselves, man is, in a sense, constantly conversing with himself."

That is a wise observation. The more advanced man becomes and the more complex his man-made environment grows, the more highly symbolized his world becomes. Eventually he tends to move away from practical concerns and to become increasingly preoccupied with abstractions of his own creation. Religious ritual, for example, becomes more important than picking beans. That is, it *seems* to be more important, and assumes a more elevated place in the thinking of the influential and sophisticated members of a society. No longer a bean picker himself, a man takes that job for granted: he leaves it to lowlier members of society and devotes his heavy thinking to more profound matters.

These tendencies are already detectable in Cycladic man. He was accustomed not only to thinking but to acting symbolically. For one thing, his economic activities began to require it. If a chief on one of the islands was going to function as the collector and dispenser of goods, and particularly if long custom was going to dictate the fairness of how he did it—so much to this man for performing such-and-such a service, so much to another for an inherited right—then there had to be ways of keeping all those transactions straight, especially if they involved storage for a considerable time or deferred payment.

In short, record keeping was necessary. And although Cycladic man could neither read nor write —in fact, had no writing system whatsoever—it can be assumed that he could keep records of some sort and, equally important, measure things with a fair degree of accuracy. Ownership was indicated by the use of seals, each engraved with the owner's private device. Traces of a numerical system appear on pots. And although the use of weights in the early Cyclades has not been established directly, it has been in Troy II, which was contemporary with Early Cycladic culture. Schliemann found pairs of silver bars that so closely matched each other in weight that their use as standard measures was obvious. Four of them, in fact, even after 4,000 years of partial oxidation, varied by only about one tenth of an ounce. For an illiterate people, this bespeaks an impressive degree of sophistication.

Measuring pops up in another area: in religion. The small stone figurines that are perhaps the greatest single artistic contribution of the Cyclades are, according to the American scholar Dr. Patricia Preziosi, carved to very precise proportions of head to torso and torso to legs. They are the earliest-known art objects in which this regularity of proportion is attempted, and as such they foreshadow the later Classical Greek statues with their emphasis on mathematical harmony.

The significance of the proportions is not understood. In fact the figurines themselves are not understood. They represent one of the great conundrums of the Aegean Bronze Age. They occur throughout the islands, but nowhere else except as imports from the Cyclades. They have their descent from more primitive neolithic forms, but in the hands of Cycladic craftsmen they emerge as slender little nude figures, mostly females, of an extreme Brancusi-like simplicity and an unearthly beauty that greatly excites art lovers today. This was not always so.

When the head shown on page 38 was discovered by a German archeologist in 1885, he described it as "repulsively ugly."

The Cycladic figurines range in size from about two inches to nearly five feet, the larger (and scarcer) ones being the earliest freestanding monumental sculptures ever made in Europe. They have enormous dignity. Their heads are oval, smoothly slanted, usually with only a nose delineated, but sometimes the outline of a mouth. None of them has incised eyes. A few of the figurines are of musicians—a seated lyre player or a standing flute player. But the most common type by far is a standing figure with folded arms. The arms are never crossed, but held against the chest, the right arm habitually below the left.

What are they? What is the significance of that pose? No one really knows. That they were highly valued is clear, since most of the figurines have been found in tombs along with other prized possessions of the deceased. Also, some had been broken and then carefully mended, indicating that they were prized during their owners' lifetimes.

Were they goddesses, images to be worshiped in their own right? Perhaps, though the suspicion is that they were not. More likely they were votive figures, privately owned images, cherished by individuals and buried with them when they died, much as a crucifix or rosary might be buried with its owner today. Possession of a figurine might even have been a mark of status, as ownership of a Botticelli madonna was for a Medici prince: a subtle mixture of conspicuous personal display and religious devotion.

But such speculation is very shaky. The truth is that next to nothing is known of the religion of the Cycladic world. In common with the Mycenaeans and

Minoans, the islanders did not go in for large temples or idols. Their religion was a small-scale, personal matter. Certain birds and trees seem to have had a sacred significance. But who the Cycladic gods were, their names and attributes, or how they were worshiped, is not known.

It might seem that there was a good deal of preoccupation with the afterlife, on the evidence of the increases in valuables that were buried with the dead. But even this conclusion is probably wrong. From all that can be deduced about the flavor of Bronze Age Aegean life, with its growing emphasis on status and wealth, it seems more likely that the valuables were put there as a mark of esteem for what a man had been while alive. A Viking chief was buried with his sword and his faithful hound, the implication being that no one else was worthy to wield the one or command the other. Similarly with a weapon or a drinking cup in a Cycladic grave; the owner had quaffed from that cup—perhaps mightily—in his life and no one else would do so after his death.

Judging by the treasures found by Schliemann at Troy II and at Mycenae, we can infer that an enormous hoard of valuables was steadily being taken out of circulation as the rich and great died—providing a fine incentive for craftsmen and traders to replace the items, and an equal incentive for grave robbers to steal them, which explains why so few of the objects survive today.

One last and surprising discovery in the Cycladic graves is a hint of the beginnings of economic snobbery. In the tombs of the rich there is usually a good deal of pottery, most of it of high quality. But there was an enormous production of plainer pots that are common in more modest graves but almost entirely lacking in the more splendid ones. It is as if the latter were saying: "We are a cut above that stuff. Let the common people use it if they like."

For the present, not a great deal more can be said about the Cyclades. The islands were cultural boomlets getting underway in a world where parallel cultures were also fermenting on mainland Greece and on Minoan Crete. It was the latter island that closed the book on the continuance of an independent Cycladic cultural tradition.

Crete, with its larger, richer valleys, its forests, its miles of vineyards and olive groves, continued to grow. Mightier barons emerged. Minoan ships appeared with superior pottery, better jewelry, handsomer bronze weapons—and, presumably, more muscle. The native Cycladic styles succumbed to this cultural onslaught and largely lost their identity. After 1700 B.C. most of the Cycladic islands were, to all intents and purposes, "Minoanized."

The islands that were most strongly influenced would at last begin to reveal, in the details of their newer frescoes and in their more elaborately decorated pottery and metalwork, something of the look of Late Cycladic society—a clue or two about how the people dressed, how they saw themselves. But before the Minoan cultural takeover, that kind of close-in look is impossible. For any feel at all for the large hopes and aspirations, the small vanities and satisfactions, the human attitudes, the sweating and dying that went on in those little islands for more than a thousand years, we have only the earlier pottery and the foundation stones of ruined buildings as a guide. And, of course, those enigmatic figurines. But they say precious little.

Enigmas Shaped in Marble

The marble figures that were buried in Third Millennium Cycladic graves represent the most baffling single puzzle of the many that cloud insight into the Aegean Bronze Age. Some scholars think the figurines were idols, and that their purpose was to invoke the protection of a goddess or to ward off her wrath. Others see them variously as personal toys, as status symbols, as soul companions for the dead. Still others, noting the large preponderance of female figures, think they may have been placed in the graves of men to satisfy their sexual desires after death. Coming from a society that was still rather primitive, and probably strongly influenced by spells, magic and fear of the dead, the sculptures may even have been embodiments of the dead, securely buried to ensure that the transient flesh would not return to haunt the living.

No theory really satisfies. Too many of the idols first fell into the hands of grave robbers, who of course did not trouble to record details of the finds before selling their loot.

The earliest Cycladic figurines were crude violin-shaped females with long necks. Most scholars agree that they derive from an older neolithic tradition that was widespread in the pre-Bronze Age Aegean for thousands of years. The one at right is five inches high, comes from the island of Despotiko and dates from about 3000 B.C.

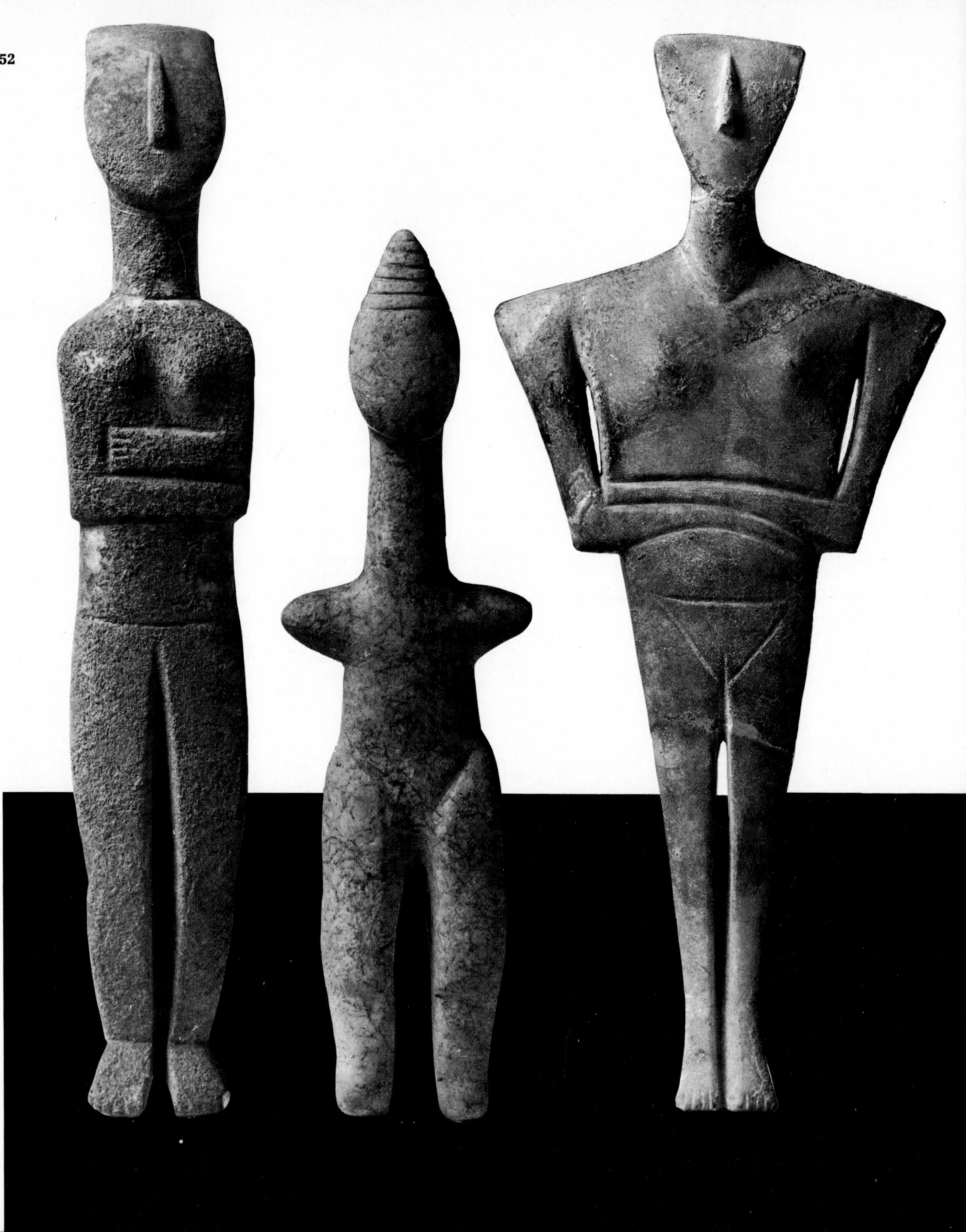

These six sculptures, ranging in size from seven to 18 inches, are examples of two other major styles of Cycladic figurines. Most popular from 3000 to 2500 B.C., the Louros type (second, fourth and sixth from left)—with its characteristic stumpy arms and legs, and minimal facial features—is comparatively primitive. The other three are folded-arm figurines and are from a later period—2500 to 1900 B.C. The figures are usually female, with prominent noses, and arms across the chest, left arm above the right.

54

Among the rarest of the Cycladic sculptures is a tiny group representing male musicians. At left is a man blowing a double flute; below and at right are two views of a seated lyre player. Both figures were unearthed on the island of Keros and are about eight inches high. Though of approximately the same age as the folded-arm type shown on the previous pages, the musician pieces are more ambitious as works of art.

Chapter Three: Crete and the Minoans

If the Bronze Age Cyclades provide only a frustratingly fragmentary picture of themselves—through having left not very much behind, and that little viewed through the darkening glass of four or five thousand years of time—it is with an entirely different kind of frustration that we approach the Minoans. They offer far more, archeologically, but all that richness delivers less than it appears to.

The Minoans were both older and younger than the Cycladic islanders; they arrived on their much larger island earlier and their culture lasted longer, leaving an unparalleled treasure behind. They came to Crete in about 7000 B.C., presumably from Asia Minor. Succeeding waves may have come later. Some authorities think they spoke an Indo-European language, which, if true, would make them vaguely, if not immediately, related to both their mainland and Cycladic neighbors. Although the Minoans learned to read and write some time after 2000 B.C. and left specimens of their writing behind, it is yet to be deciphered; their language remains an enigma. In the end we are left wondering who they were and where they came from.

They are a people tantalizing in the extreme. Extraordinarily gifted architects, unmatched as potters, the developers of a fresh realistic style of fresco painting that has no counterpart anywhere else in the world, they transmit to us through their works a vivid picture of a talented, subtle, luxury-loving, worldly and obviously highly sophisticated people.

They were very responsive to the natural world—to flowers, animals, birds, fish. They loved scenery. With the single exception of Knossos, they placed their palaces and particularly their country villas so that they had commanding views of the countryside, down mountains or out across the sea. Their preoccupation with plumbing and bathtubs (page 77) makes it clear that they were very clean. They admired the human body and had their own standards of physical beauty.

Men and women alike, in the pictures they made of themselves, were slender, with long graceful limbs and extremely narrow waists. The men were broad-shouldered, often depicted wearing only loincloths. The women wore full-length flounced skirts and tight bodices open at the front to reveal firm, full breasts. They loved jewelry and fancy hairdos. They also loved athletics: boxing and a sport peculiar to them that involved acrobatics with bulls.

They were a religious people, but not oppressively so. There seems to have been little that was dark or cruel in their faith. Although the bronze swords, daggers and spear points that have turned up in their graves give good evidence that they were fighters, they do not seem to have been a notably aggressive people, certainly they were not in their later years; their art is almost totally lacking in representations of battles or of killing.

All in all, they come across as a charming people of a remarkably modern temper, almost dainty in their style. Looking at the archeological testament they left, we feel a strong affinity for them—and a sense that if we could get one step closer, we could really get to know them.

A masterpiece from Knossos, this eight-inch bull's-head rhyton—or ceremonial vessel—is carved of black stone and the nostril edges are inlaid with white shell. The white-crystal eyes, with their bright-red painted pupils, achieve a startlingly fiery effect. The horns, lost but here restored, were probably made of wood and then covered with gold foil.

Models of Minoan houses were found by Arthur Evans at Knossos, and gave him clues as to what the houses of ordinary people looked like. The models (shown here actual size) were employed as decorative inlays for a wooden chest. They are made of faïence, i.e., clay objects to which varicolored opaque glazes are applied and then fired.

That last step is the difficult one. The Minoans are the only literate, highly civilized people in the world who appear to have had no sense of history whatsoever. Names and dates meant so little to them that they left no single written record that includes either. As a result, vivid though the Minoans may be in those aspects of themselves that they do reveal, in every other they are totally impersonal. In the end they emerge as two-dimensional: elegant, graceful, humorous—but enigmatic.

If there were a single real man—a Solomon, a Pericles, an Akhenaton, a Nebuchadnezzar, a Darius —one flesh-and-blood personality warmed by lusts and conquests, cooled by failures, who could be squeezed out of a couple of thousand years of Minoan history, that disembodied impersonal feeling might go away. But there is none. The Minoans, from the moment they appear on the world stage to the moment they depart from it, remain anonymous.

The very choice of the name Minoan is questionable. It was bestowed on the culture in 1904 by Arthur Evans, who got it from one of the rare names traceable to Crete that he could discover in all the myths told by the Greeks. That was Minos, possibly not a man's name at all but a title. It was a bold stroke to hang an entire civilization on such a flimsy hook, but Minoan name-hooks are scarce. The Egyptians called the Minoans Keftiu; what they called themselves we have no idea.

Of one thing we can be sure: the Minoans were remarkably innovative artists. Their art is utterly beguiling in its emphasis on nature. It is full of twining plants, blooming flowers, leaping dolphins, wriggling octopuses, fluttering swallows, prancing ibexes. So divorced is their art from their history and their politics that one begins to wonder if the omissions do not reflect some strict esthetic canon that scorned such mundane things as the loading of ships, the storming of cities, the flaying of captured enemies, the tribute-bringing and abasement of vassal princes. All these subjects were major themes in the art of other great states contemporary with Minoan culture, memorializing the pride of the arrogant kings who commissioned it.

The Minoans were utterly unlike those other peoples. If they were arrogant, they were so in ways they do not reveal to us. Can the picture they leave of themselves—preoccupied with sports, with sunny religious practices, with processions and dancing, with the beauties of the natural world—be a kind of put-on, a picture of a society of flower children? Surely not. They were hardworking and prosperous, able craftsmen, shrewd traders, experienced sailors, and their influence in the Aegean is obvious even while the extent of their dominance is still being debated.

Was the Aegean and all its islands a private Minoan lake? Did the Minoan control constitute a thalassocracy, making Crete the world's first true sea power—with a fleet and a maritime policy that enforced Minoan will on all its neighbors?

That is very hard to say. Archeological research has revealed that the southernmost of the Cyclades, Thera, was a Minoan colony; and that another island to the west, Kythera, was one too. Minoan artifacts have been found on Cycladic Melos and Kea, on Rhodes in the eastern Aegean and finally at Miletus on the coast of Asia Minor. The manufactured goods of the Minoans went everywhere. There is no question that their power and influence were formidable. But throughout much of the Aegean their strength

seems to have been exercised more as the result of an overwhelmingly potent cultural stimulus than direct political control.

That same stimulus spread to the Greek mainland and was so strong by about 1600 B.C. that some scholars became convinced it was explicable only in terms of Minoan dominion there. Arthur Evans thought so. Others disagreed, pointing out that the mainlanders were themselves powerful people, more warlike than the Minoans and more than able to hold their own on their home territory. One of the dissenters was Alan Wace, head of the British School of Archaeology at Athens. He was a great authority on Mycenae and devoted much of his life to studying mainland sites. His view brought him into direct conflict with the all-powerful Evans. At the time Evans prevailed, but today's scholarship, more and more, is vindicating Wace.

What may well have been the most important Minoan political contribution to the Aegean world was the elimination of piracy. It seems likely that the Minoans were determined, in their own trading interest, to have peace in the Aegean, and put an end to the buccaneering. If they did, their influence as tranquilizers probably began to be felt by 2000 B.C. By 1700 B.C. they had become dominant in the area—so dominant that they appear never to have had any fears themselves of piratical attack. Unlike the Cycladic towns, which had to become heavily fortified to survive, the great Minoan palaces had no fortifications whatsoever. The only possible conclusion to be reached about this strange circumstance is that their occupants felt so secure in their naval superiority that they considered fortifications a waste of energy.

However, that does not dispose of a still stranger question: Why did not the Minoans fight among themselves? After about 2000 B.C. fairly dense populations were beginning to concentrate around five or six main power centers on Crete. These were just beginning to emerge as palace complexes and were due for an enormous growth in size and opulence over the next 300 years. The largest of the palaces was at Knossos, but there was another of impressive size and wealth at Mallia not far away, and an even more luxurious one at Phaistos on the south coast, across the island from Knossos. Given the worldwide predilection of men to covet and to fight, how can the failure of a rich plum like Phaistos to protect itself with fortifications be explained?

Three possibilities suggest themselves:

First, the assumption can be made that they *did* fight one another, but for reasons unknown chose not to fortify. If that theory is correct, its justification may lie in some lost code of behavior, mixed possibly with religion, in which fighting of only a certain kind was tolerated—perhaps waged only by a warrior class. A victory would have been acknowledged on the field, after which a relatively sober and bloodless series of concessions might have been made by the losing side.

Canceling this rather lofty view is some evidence of sporadic damage to the early sites (other than that caused by earthquakes, to be discussed later), indicating that fighting did indeed take place and was occasionally accompanied by its share of burning and destruction during the earlier centuries of Minoan cultural upthrust. Such damage adds mystery to the apparent perversity of the rulers in their decision not to fortify their palaces better.

A second scenario suggests that the Minoans did not fight among themselves, presumably because one palace was acknowledged as the overlord of the others. If that was so, then, on the basis of sheer size, the overlord was almost certainly Knossos. However, such a picture of peaceful coexistence under a single authority does not contradict the possibility that there was earlier turbulence.

Finally, it can be argued that the Minoans did not fight among themselves because—though there may not have been a dominant Knossos to prevent confrontations—it was in the mutual interest of all not to do so. This mutuality could have been based on some sort of island-wide network of religious control and/or economic interdependence.

Mutual interest brings us back to the role of the redistributive center, identified by Colin Renfrew as critical to the development of both the Cycladic and Minoan cultures. The Cyclades, it should be remembered, failed to get beyond a certain point in their upward cultural thrust because of their small size. No such restraint existed on Crete; the centralization of power, bureaucracy and wealth kept right on increasing until something new in the Aegean world—palace economies—emerged, grew larger and ultimately became the pivots around which all Minoan society revolved. Everything that went on in a Minoan state was probably directed from the palace. Great hoards of grain and oil were stored there. The impetus for the arts was centered there. Crafts flourished there. Wealth was concentrated there. All favor and privilege were dispensed from there. In short, the redistributive system itself, in its developed palace form, could have been a deterrent to warfare.

Who ran the large multiroomed palaces—who did

About 25 feet in diameter, a tholos at Kamilari on Crete is one of the largest ever found. Like all these Minoan tombs, it had been plundered of its most valuable grave goods.

One item thieves missed at Kamilari is a baked-clay model, nine inches high, of four male dancers with peaked caps. The horns of consecration around the model's base suggest that a dance of this kind may have been performed outside the tholos as a religious ritual.

Where the Minoans Buried Their Dead

One of the most remarkable features of Minoan culture is the tholos tomb. Nearly 80 of the low, round stone structures have been discovered, most of them in the Mesara Plain near Phaistos. Their walls are heavy, and they curve inward as they rise, suggesting that they were vaulted. However, since all the roofs have fallen in, it is not possible to tell whether they had true domes or whether they were topped by flat wooden coverings. But it is certain that they were used communally. All seem to have been next to settlements; and most are very old, dating from as early as 2800 B.C., long before the rise of the palace-states. They were used again and again—gradually filled up with skeletons and grave goods, then periodically cleaned out, fumigated, a new earth floor laid down and the process repeated. Some tholoi were in continuous use for more than a thousand years.

A second model from Kamilari, just four inches high, re-creates a Minoan scene. Seated in a room with columns and windows are four important individuals, each being treated to a libation by a servant. It may be that the larger figures are deities and the smaller ones their religious attendants.

the distributing—is another mystery. Whether the occupants were kings, god-kings, queens, goddess-queens, whether there were ruling high priests (or priestesses) who exercised their power by divine right through a bureaucracy of lesser priests or nobles is not known for sure. What does appear to be almost certain is that Minoan society was highly stratified, with the duties and perquisites of each layer spelled out in some detail. So long as it is reasonably bearable by all classes, such a structure makes for an extremely stable society. If everyone's place in life is determined from birth, and if there is a crushing weight of tradition to force acceptance of things as they are, then there will be a minimum of unrest at all levels, unless the system is subjected to some unacceptable strain.

At the bottom there is neither hope nor precedent for advancement. At the top the lucky ones who are already there are glad to stay, and can be counted on to make every effort they can to solidify the existing traditions of government and religion that serve to maintain the status quo.

In the middle—well, there may or may not have been a middle level. Traditionally the middle classes have provided the ferment that shakes up a society. They are the tradesmen, the entrepreneurs and the artisans who, by the gradual accumulation of wealth, begin to have aspirations for higher social status. Since Crete was industrially productive and engaged in widespread trade, clearly somewhere in Minoan society there existed groups to carry out that work. But they may have been regarded by the nobility as merely the "top of the bottom." However strenuous and useful the activities of artist or trader or entrepreneur may have been, their output still would have

been channeled through the palace—much or all of it becoming, in effect, the property of the palace: just another part of the centrally monitored economic machine that, in the end, determined the fortunes and stations of all.

Alternatively, if the hierarchy of priests and nobles was large, with numerous levels, many of the duties and privileges that normally would fall to a middle class in another society may have been absorbed by that large and flexible aristocracy. In short, there may have been a kind of "bottom of the top": a large bureaucracy of lesser nobles, a world of limited, splintered, carefully described and jealously guarded privileges whose effect would have been to freeze the status quo.

All the foregoing is speculative. But it seems to provide the most satisfactory explanation of why the Minoan cities were not fortified. The "haves" continued to have and were not about to rock the boat; the "have-nots" were persuaded by custom, by religion or by force not to do so.

Also, living conditions for everyone during the best days of the palaces may have been so good as to blunt any incentive for either civil unrest or warfare. The carrying capacity of a society—the number of people it can support in tolerable comfort—is determined by how efficiently it is set up to get the maximum yield from the land, the maximum output from the potter and so on. At the heart of the matter is the society's ability to distribute things effectively. For its day the palace redistributive system must have been a marvel of efficiency.

With all the Minoan cities functioning in this way —active in agriculture, in manufacturing and the arts, extending their trade powerfully overseas—it simply

Text continued on page 66

Details of the Great Palace at Knossos

The south anteroom is one of the most thoroughly restored portions of the palace: rebuilt walls, new columns and a fresco in place.

Arthur Evans was not content to excavate, clean up, analyze and remove to museums all the material he found at Knossos. Realizing that to do so would leave not much more than an impersonal tracery of low walls and foundations, he determined to recapture something of the look of the palace as it actually had been.

He therefore set about reassembling walls, propping them up with concrete and stone members, making columns identical to the original ones, even going so far as to put some heavily restored frescoes on the walls. Although he has been criticized for some mistakes he made, there is no doubt that a sense of what a Minoan palace looked like is stronger at Knossos than at any other Cretan site.

The restoration above is a fine example of Evans' work. The walls have been rebuilt to ceiling height. Reinforcing beams (originally wood) have been installed. Doorways and steps have been re-created—and a Minoan palace emerges out of thin air.

The queen's megaron at Knossos—the principal sitting room in her suite—has a fresco of fishes and dolphins. The border below it, framing a door, had originally been painted with rosettes and, later, was painted over with spirals. Arthur Evans left parts of both designs showing. The door under the fresco led to the king's quarters.

A section of ceiling from one of the royal residential rooms on the east side of the palace had fallen into a lower room where it was found in pieces. Its raised stucco spirals are overlaid with red, blue and yellow rosettes.

The "throne of Minos" is made of stone, and sits where Arthur Evans found it, along the wall of a dark chamber that may have been used either for religious or state functions. The throne, the floor and some of the stone benches that line the walls are authentic; the walls are restored with griffin frescoes based on surviving fragments.

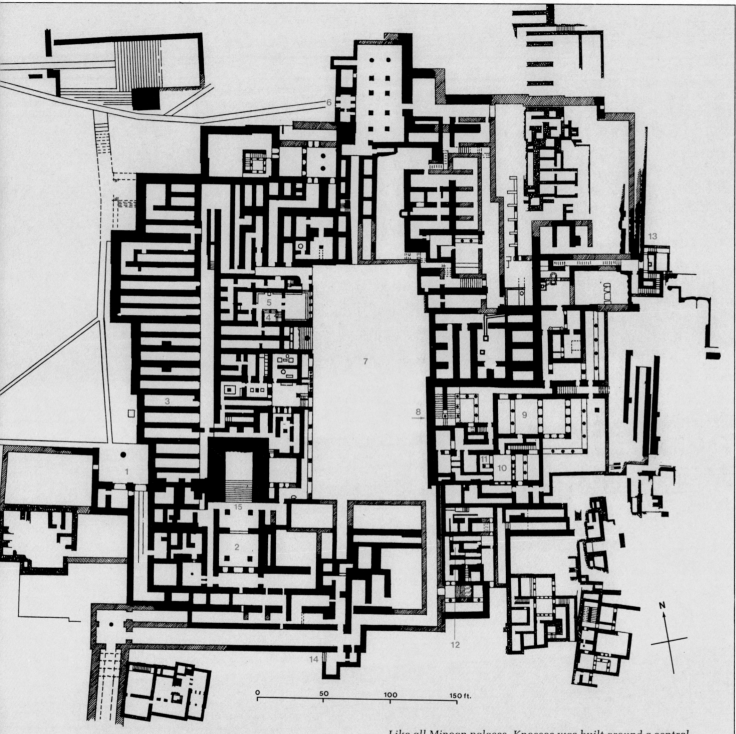

1. West entrance
2. South anteroom
3. West storerooms
4. Lustral chamber
5. Throne room
6. North entrance
7. Central court
8. Grand staircase
9. King's megaron
10. Queen's megaron
11. Queen's bath
12. Shrine of the Double Axes
13. East entrance
14. South entrance
15. Staircase to second story

Like all Minoan palaces, Knossos was built around a central court. The royal apartments were to the east, storage rooms to the west. The so-called throne room, which may in fact have been a shrine, was a few steps down to the west of the court. The public rooms for state business were also to the west, on a second story. A visitor today enters through a western portal. A key to a tour of the palace is at left.

may not have been in their interest to engage in local squabbles at home. If the entire island be considered as a very large redistributive system, its parts interlocking to the mutual benefit of all, then there would have been no more incentive for Knossos to fight with Phaistos than there would be for New York to fight with New Jersey.

A final interesting suggestion on this point has been made by J. W. Graham of the University of Toronto. He points out that the strong naval forces of the Minoans and their remoteness from other powers made their island virtually immune to invasion for a thousand years, and perhaps for much longer. This situation would have produced an unusually homogeneous population with a far better chance of living in peace with itself than the rest of the world's mixed-up, ethnically jangled, eternally moving, squabbling and rebellious peoples.

Whatever the reason, the palace centers, once they began to develop in about 2000 B.C., apparently managed to get along in remarkable harmony that lasted for more than 500 years and was interrupted only by a sudden calamity that overtook them all. Evidence of a disaster began to reveal itself to Evans when he first started excavating at Knossos. The deeper he dug into that labyrinthine place, the clearer it became that something terrible had struck it. Walls had toppled, ceilings had come crashing down, there was evidence of appalling fire.

What could have happened? Evans did not know, nor could he even guess when it had happened. He was dealing with an enormous palace of unknown age, unknown style, unknown dimensions, whose nature and purpose were at first indecipherable by him since it had been conceived by an unknown people of unknown habits.

His problem was complicated by the fact that major sections of the palace had been built and rebuilt over many hundreds of years and were now in a hideous jumble. Parts of it had stood four or five stories high. When its floors had collapsed, pottery had gone plunging into basements, along with clay tablets and other objects. Walls had crashed, their stones raised at some later date for the building of new walls, then, still later, crashed again.

Furthermore, Evans was laboring under a misconception that only a growing familiarity with Knossos would erase. It must be remembered that he had gone there originally only in search of seal stones, those exquisite little gems with their cryptic carvings. He was interested in languages and in the hints of an unknown writing system, perhaps related in some way to the hieroglyphic signs of Egypt, that were engraved on those Minoan seals.

But when he first began to find pottery at Knossos he recognized instantly that it bore a strong resemblance to pots found at Mycenae and other places on the Greek mainland. Knowing nothing yet of the true dimensions of Minoan culture, he followed the only scholarly line that was possible at the time. He assumed that the pots were Mycenaean exports, and so stated in his early letters and reports. It would only gradually dawn on him that he was dealing with a culture far greater, older, more sophisticated than, and basically different from, the Mycenaean.

Even as he was juggling this wild surmise—probing deeper, his vision expanding at express-train speed—he hit on another problem: Knossos, the continuing excavations revealed, had been destroyed not once but twice, the second calamity happening some hundreds of years after the first. Compounding the riddle of who the Minoans were, where they came from, when they lived, how they had evolved such a magnificent civilization, was this added conundrum, equally opaque: What had caused the *two* disasters? Finally, and perhaps the most puzzling of all, what had become of the Minoans?

To begin to answer these questions, Evans had to solve—or at least to make educated guesses about —half a dozen related matters. Architectural clues as to which of the chambers were royal suites, which were throne rooms, which were shrines, had to be strengthened by other clues coming from gem seals and frescoes that pictured Minoan men and women engaged in all sorts of activities ranging from acrobatics to religious observances. Each unit in the expanding intellectual structure had to draw support from the others. Gradually a coherent edifice arose, anchored in time to contemporary events from better-known places outside Crete, notably Egypt. The chart on page 21 is a recent version of Evans' final view of the Minoan world. What it says, in brief, is that Minoan culture can be divided into three main periods, based on changes in the sequence of pottery styles that Evans had worked out.

Early Minoan—corresponding roughly to the Cycladic—was, with all of its subdivisions and its sub-subdivisions, an Early Bronze Age culture, emerging from the neolithic. It extended from about 3000 B.C. to about 2000 B.C.

Thereafter, according to Evans, there was a considerable rise in the level of social and cultural organization on Crete. A big palace began to grow at Knossos. The multiplier effect was obviously at work.

The population was increasing rapidly. Agriculture, manufacturing and trade were carrying Knossos to a level that had never been reached on the smaller Cycladic islands. Evans gave this second period the name Middle Minoan, and dated it from 2000 to 1600 B.C. Later scholars have disagreed with Evans—and among themselves—about that time fix. A good compromise, based on the most recent archeological interpretations, would seem to place the Middle Minoan period at 2000 to 1500 B.C.

Toward the end of the Middle Minoan period, in about 1700 B.C., this rush of progress was interrupted. The palace at Knossos fell in ruins for the first time. Was it sacked—exploding the idea of peaceful coexistence among Minoan cities? Apparently not, as a larger look at Crete would reveal.

In the early years of the 20th Century, on the heels of Evans, other archeologists from France, America, England, Italy and Greece, fanned out over Crete. Quite quickly they began finding the sites of other palace complexes and handsome villas scattered over the central and eastern parts of the island. Like Knossos, these palaces, too, had been destroyed. Pottery sequencing, confirmed by more modern dating techniques, has indicated that this island-wide palace collapse took place all in one blow.

Since there was no evidence of foreign invasion —and no possibility of it, considering the limited development of the Cyclades and mainland Greece at the time, not to mention the great unlikelihood that a bunch of invaders would succeed in battering down palaces scores of miles apart in simultaneous attacks —logic compelled the view that the first catastrophe had been the result of an earthquake. Evans, in fact, stated quite early his belief that this was the case.

A trio of Minoan girls, known as the Ladies in Blue, chat animatedly at a public event. They are wearing the breast-baring boleros that were fashionable among the high born.

A Revealing Glimpse of the Ancient Minoans

Exacty what the Minoans looked like remained a blank until 1900, when Arthur Evans began finding bits of wall paintings at Knossos. The colors were still bright despite the passage of time. As Evans set about reassembling the fragments, one of the first facts to become apparent was an artistic convention: the skin color for males was always red; that for females, white. The frescoes also revealed what the Minoans wore and how they saw themselves—as slender, graceful people with narrow waists. Both sexes took pains with their hair, letting it grow long and then arranging it in thick curls that fell in front of their ears.

Perhaps most charming of all the Minoan faces in the Knossos frescoes is this 10-inch fragment of a girl with large doe eyes and ringlets. Her chic and modernity have earned her the name La Parisienne.

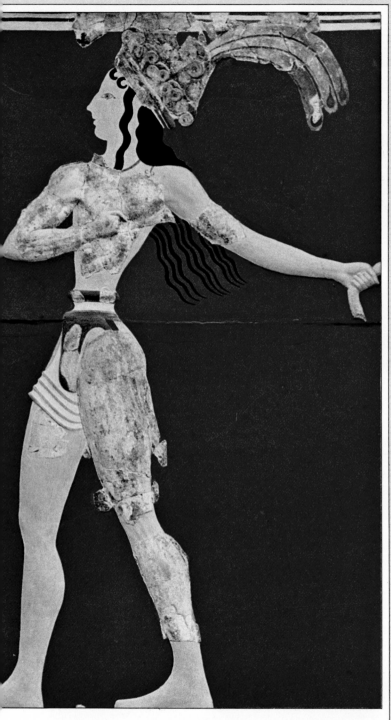

Clad in light summer garb, this striding youth wears a belt around his slim waist, a kilt and a codpiece—and nothing else except an elaborate headdress. The figure has been tentatively identified as a priest-king, but no one knows for sure who he was. Life-sized, he is pulling something with his left hand; whatever it was might have supplied a clue to his identity, but unfortunately that vital part of the fresco has been lost.

His explanation is now universally accepted. Crete has had a long history of earthquakes, some of them extremely severe.

Furthermore, social rot or unrest would not account for the smash, because the Minoans picked themselves up after the disaster and with great vigor rebuilt their palaces on an even larger and more luxurious scale than before. Evidently, at this stage in Minoan history, the social and economic forces that had produced the palace economies were not faltering in any way; in 1700 B.C. the multiplier effect was still operative and Minoan influence continued to grow in the Aegean. The point must be stressed because that situation may well have been different some 250 years later, at the time of a second destruction of the palaces.

The third and final phase of the civilization identified by Evans was given the name Late Minoan. It ran from about 1500 B.C. to about 1100 B.C., by which time it had dwindled away to nothing. At this point it should be emphasized that though there was an overall pattern of increasing richness in Minoan culture as it developed, the adjectives early, middle and late should not be interpreted to mean steady improvements from one period to the next. The words are arbitrary and based entirely on changes in pottery styles. Actually, Minoan culture began to peak with the rebuilding of the palaces after the great earthquake in, roughly, 1700 B.C. It remained in full bloom until after the second palace-collapse, which occurred about 1450 B.C.

The palace complex was obviously a brilliant invention, overwhelmingly successful for its time and its society. Just how it functioned is not quite so obvious. Beyond question, it was an intricate bureau-

Faïence figures from Knossos prove there was a religious association between Minoan goddesses and snakes. This deity is festooned with three reptiles: one is wriggling up her right arm, around her neck and down her left; another starts at her waist, edges past her breast to her ear; a third spirals down her conical headdress to wrap its tail around her waist.

cracy, highly centralized, highly institutionalized. But who the bureaucrats were and, particularly, who stood at the very top has not been established. Most authorities suspect that the ruler may have been a priest-king of some type.

Minoan art makes clear the populace's great preoccupation with religion. The murals, and particularly the small engraved gem seals and gold finger rings, depict over and over again what are believed to be religious observances of one sort or another. Despite this preoccupation, public temples or other large centers of worship were missing from the Minoan world. Instead, there were shrines—small holy rooms with altars—tucked away in many palace locations. The consequence was to transform the entire palace at Knossos into a religious center and to make the authority that flowed from it—that of a priest-king—a powerful blend of the secular and the religious.

Quite early in his investigations at Knossos, Evans began finding the ruins of frescoes. Some remained isolated fragments, but others, though broken into hundreds of tiny bits, have been laboriously reassembled. They give the modern world the first good look at Minoan faces. And what faces they are! The Minoans seem to have borrowed from Egyptian artistic traditions in that they tended to show countenances in profile, shoulders and torsos head-on. But their departure from Egyptian—or any other—artistic influence was immediate and profound. There is a stiffness to Egyptian art, a formality, that is totally avoided in the ebullient Minoan frescoes.

One of the finest discovered by Evans centers on the full-length figure of a young man thought to represent a priest-king (page 69). He is a magnificent

A second goddess holds a wriggling snake in each hand. Both figurines are dressed alike, in the fashion followed by highborn Minoan women: tight bodice open at the front, heavy pleated skirt and an apron of some sort hanging down from the waist. The names of the goddesses, their divine attributes, the significance of the snakes remain a mystery.

creature—slender, well-muscled, clad in a codpiece (the abbreviated loincloth or athletic supporter affected by Minoan men) and a small kilt, with a heavy belt around his wasp waist. On his head is an extraordinary plumed headdress. He is shown striding through a field of lilies and butterflies, one arm extended behind him as though carrying or pulling something. His other arm, with fist clenched, is doubled across his chest. His entire being seems to vibrate with an unearthly blend of grace and force.

Contrast the priest-king to another Evans find: the so-called *Ladies in Blue* fresco (page 68). Part of a larger work, this fresco shows three young women of the court sitting together, apparently gossiping as they watch an event of some sort—a procession, a court function or an entertainment. Wearing elaborate boleros, open in front to reveal their breasts, festooned with necklaces and bracelets, their hair curled and freighted with ropes of beads, they make a charming group. Their heads are turned this way and that as they talk, their hands fluttering in the most elegant and refined gestures imaginable.

Here, in contrast to the power radiating from the priest-king fresco, is the essence of frivolity and feminine charm. No society that did not admire women and give them a great deal of freedom could possibly have created such a work. That women were so admired is indicated over and over again by the discovery of other frescoes showing literally dozens of charming ladies, all similarly clad, all gesturing with a gracious artificiality reminiscent of the French court in the days of Fragonard or Boucher. In fact, one fragment, the face of a delicious minx with a retroussé nose, has come to be known as *La Parisienne* for her beguiling expression and her chic.

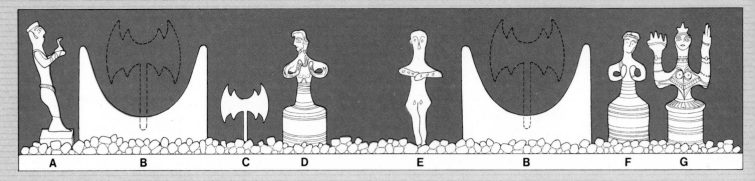

A   B   C   D   E   B   F   G

But women were not mere ornaments, admired for their beauty and grace. They appear to have held a remarkably emancipated position in Minoan society. They mingled freely with men, as they would not do even in progressive Athens a thousand or more years later. They figured prominently in religion, both as worshipers and priestesses. The chief Minoan deity turns out to have been a goddess.

Goddesses appear again and again on seal stones —slender figures in flounced skirts and with streaming hair—often attended by priestesses, sometimes by men. Often the goddess is depicted with a dove or a snake, both creatures being sacred to her. There is no dodging the importance of the snake in the Minoan culture, though its specific significance is obscure. It appears on seals and pottery, as well as on figurines of goddesses.

Female deities have been found in the several small shrines—none more than four or five feet square—of the Knossos palace complex. One in particular, known as the Shrine of the Double Axes, is remarkably interesting and revealing. It is built on three levels, rising a step at a time as one penetrates it. At the first level are some jugs and vases, presumably used for liquid offerings. The second level features a small three-legged stool coated with plaster. Small cups and jugs surround it. Presumably offerings were to be placed there and libations poured.

The rearmost, and highest, section of the shrine was devoted to the goddess herself. It was dominated by two sets of horns of consecration: saddle-like clay structures with a stucco surface (page 72). In the dip of the saddle, between each pair of horns, was a hole—a socket to hold the sacred double ax.

Double axes, while undoubtedly used in combat and as work tools, were stylized and reduced in size when designed for Minoan shrines—no longer weapons but delicate symbols, often made of gold. Their incorporation into the cult probably resulted from their having been used initially to kill sacrifical animals. The late Swedish scholar Martin Nilsson, a world authority on Minoan religion, compared the double ax with the cross of Christianity and the crescent of Islam. Thus, it would have been the symbol of Minoan religion generally, rather than that of any specific deity.

It is worth noting that the double-ax symbol appears over and over again carved or scratched into the stones of the palace walls, emphasizing the impression that the entire place was deemed holy, saturated with the presence of the goddess and her deputy on earth, the priest-king. Also significant is the fact that the word for double ax was labrys. The word labyrinth, identifying the palace as the house of the double ax, derives from it; and so too, because of the palace's complexity, does its modern meaning, stemming from the Minotaur myth.

When Evans first opened the Shrine of the Double Axes, it actually contained a small ax made of stone and some goddess figurines of a type found commonly in other Minoan shrines. They are made of clay—females naked to the waist, arms raised at the elbow, palms sometimes turned inward, sometimes forward toward the worshiper. Some have snakes twined about their torsos, some do not. One has a dove perched on her head to signify her divinity. Such figurines are known as bell-shaped idols because, below the waist, they are formed into simple, skirtlike cylinders.

Other figurines found in the Shrine of the Double

Against the back wall of the Shrine of the Double Axes at Knossos, Arthur Evans discovered a narrow platform covered with pebbles and containing five terra-cotta figures. The illustration at left is based on his original drawings. The figure with arms raised (G) is a goddess, her status established by the dove on her head. The other skirted figures (D, F) are her attendants. The man holding a dove as an offering (A) and the nude female (E) are worshipers. The curved objects (B) are horns of consecration—each with a socket, perhaps to hold a sacred double ax (dotted outlines). One much smaller double ax (C) was actually discovered by Evans in the shrine.

Axes are not so clearly identifiable—either as goddesses or worshipers. One, however, a male figure, is obviously a worshiper; he holds the offering of a dove in his hand.

Small indoor shrines were not limited to the palaces. They have also been found in the elaborate villas that were occupied by the Minoan nobility, re-emphasizing the privacy of religious practice. It was, in large part, a home affair. It can be assumed that the simpler houses of the common people had their shrines too—perhaps nothing more than a niche or small alcove with a few holy objects in it.

Another, more public aspect of Minoan religious life took place out of doors—on mountain peaks, at rock shelters or in sacred caves. Caves are numerous on Crete and many contain stalagmites or other odd-shaped lumps of stone that were evidently singled out for worship as idols. People went to these remote places in groups to perform religious rites, including the shaking of holy trees and dancing—both of which are indicated on gem seals and rings. In addition, like all their contemporaries, the Minoans sacrificed animals. There are seal stones and frescoes showing trussed-up goats and bulls, ready to be killed. Furthermore, one cave, at Psychro in the central hills south of Mallia, has yielded up a thick stratum of animal bones, the residue of thousands of sacrifices, together with various bronze objects, including double axes and many small clay figurines of animals, notably bulls—votive offerings to the deity of the cave, substitutes for live sacrifices.

Much speculation has been devoted to the role of the bull in Minoan life. It appears in a most provocative way both in archeological finds and in many remarkable myths. Bulls, it is true, were used on Crete for sacrifice, but for that purpose they were no more holy in themselves than goats or wild game. The one sure fact about them that does emerge is almost more remarkable than the myths. Hints that there might have been some sort of ritual exercise involving Minoan youths and bulls began to show up on engraved gem seals and bits of pottery. Then Evans made another smashing find: a fresco (*page 74*) depicting a team of three young acrobats apparently turning somersaults over the back of a charging bull.

This scene is so extraordinary that at first glance it does not seem possible to take it literally. The charging bull is enormous, the human figures small. One waiting acrobat is standing directly in front of the bull, grasping its horns. Is this for the purpose of engaging the bull's attention or is it the start of an upward vault between the bull's horns, to be followed by a somersault over its back and down to the ground again behind its tail? Apparently the latter, for a second figure is in the middle of such a maneuver. He is balanced on his hands on the bull's back, his legs whirling over, his face looking anxiously to the rear, toward a third figure who stands just behind the bull, arms outstretched, ready to catch him.

Considering the murderous hook of a bull's horns and the enormous strength of its neck, can we believe that young Minoan acrobats managed this appallingly rash stunt? Particularly, can we believe it when we discover that two of the acrobats are *girls*? We know they are because, though they are clad only in the abbreviated loincloths worn by male acrobats, and though they have slender boyish figures, their skins are white. By Minoan artistic convention women were shown with white skins, men with red skins.

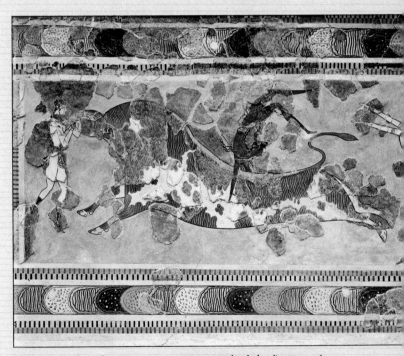

Apparently we must believe it. Enough other depictions of the same acrobatic feat by teams of youths and girls have been found to make it clear that bull-leaping was widely practiced, probably by a class of professional athletes, and watched by large audiences. But how and where it was done remains a mystery.

Conceivably the bulls were stolid animals, oxen perhaps, trained to deliver a dependable straight lift of the head to give the leaper the impetus needed to get him off the ground. But the evidence of the art denies even this explanation. Minoan artists were superb depicters of animals, and their bulls are bursting with vigor and menace.

Was bull-leaping just a sport? The British archeologist Sinclair Hood, who worked for years on Crete, thinks not. He believes the practice may have had some religious or magical significance—though others disagree with him, just as they do among themselves as to where the spectacles took place. None of the bull-leaping scenes so far discovered provides a clue as to the locations of the arenas. But every Minoan palace was built around a large open court, and it has been assumed by many that bull-leaping was conducted there. However, this theory raises problems. In at least two of the palaces (at Knossos and Mallia) the central court was entirely surrounded by a maze of royal apartments, shrines, bathrooms, reception halls, storage vaults and narrow corridors. Neither palace seems designed to accommodate an event that would require the moving about of large, dangerous animals.

Furthermore, none of the courts is large enough to permit very much in the way of maneuvering by the acrobats. One in particular, at Kato Zakro, is dangerously small and would have given little free play

This fresco, found at Knossos in 1900, supplied the first proof that Minoans staged bull-leaping events. A man (red skin) somersaults over the galloping bull's back, to be caught by a girl comrade (white skin). Another girl seizes the horns to duplicate the stunt. The 11-inch acrobat above the fresco, also from Knossos, has interlocking parts fastened by dowels.

to bull-leapers; it is about 40 feet wide and 100 feet long. The court at Mallia, though nearly twice as large, has the remains of an altar of some sort in its center—an awkward obstruction.

Finally, all the courts are paved in stone, an unforgiving surface for life-risking acrobatics. Professor Graham, who is an authority on Minoan palaces and a believer that the bull-leaping did take place in the central courts, gets around the paving problem by suggesting that the stones were sprinkled with a layer of sand before the spectacle took place—an explanation that would not seem to be entirely reasonable, since sand sprinkled over stone provides exceptionally treacherous footing.

Graham agrees with Hood that bull-leaping may have been part of religious ritual, and thinks the bull may have been sacrificed at the end of the acrobatics. If bull-leaping was a religious rite, then the theory that it took place in the palace makes better sense; inasmuch as the palace was the center of all things, it would have been involved with things holy.

Graham has another argument too, based on archeological evidence, in support of the palace-as-arena theory. He has studied the doorways that give onto the courtyards, as well as what is left of the columned porticoes that ran down their long sides, and believes that a case can be made that the audiences located in the porticoes were protected by barriers while bull-leaping was in progress.

One way to confirm that the central courts of the palaces were not used for bull-leaping is to find other sites. And that evidence may just be appearing. At Knossos a recent excavation has revealed what may be a bull ring outside the palace proper. At Mallia a large court to the north of the palace has been unearthed; scholars suspect that it, too, could have functioned as an arena. But the evidence, so far, is sketchy. Just where the bull-leapers practiced their art remains undecided.

The palaces are better at revealing other aspects of Minoan life. This is particularly true at Knossos, where Evans, early in his excavations, was forced to make a critical decision. Any archeologist working in three dimensions will have to remove important objects—and thus destroy their spatial relationship —if he wishes to dig deeper for other objects. Walls, for example, sometimes have to come down; floors have to be torn up. Evans sought a way out of this dilemma by rebuilding parts of the palace as he proceeded with his digging. For the vanished great timbers that made up ceiling beams, and for the lost wooden lintels of doors and windows, he substituted stone, steel and concrete members in the obvious locations. In this way he was able to retain some existing walls and reassemble others that had fallen down. From frescoes and column bases still in place in the palace he was able to deduce that an important feature of Minoan architecture was a round column that, unlike the Greek or the Egyptian versions, grew thicker as it rose. So he made columns of stone, and painted them red—their original color, as he knew from the frescoes.

The result has often been criticized. It is a queer blend of very ancient stone and modern concrete, some of it erroneously put together, according to the latest studies. But the pluses far outweigh the minuses. If Evans had not carried out his reconstruction, Knossos—when it had been all excavated, mapped, analyzed and swept up—to a great extent

The engineering ingenuity of Knossos architects is apparent in this photograph of the east entrance to the palace. The drainage system was constructed with baffles to slow down the heavy flow of runoff and keep it from flooding over the palace floors. The gutter along the stairs (foreground) has a series of zigzags and basins to retard the rush of water. At each landing the gutter turns a right angle, further controlling the speed of flow and conducting the water into a cistern.

Prehistoric Plumbing

To accommodate the torrential rains that fell on Crete during the autumn and spring, the palace at Knossos was constructed with separate drainage systems in each of its sections. A complex of ducts, gutters and catch basins fed into larger underground channels, with manholes at intervals for convenient access. The main channels, made of stone and lined with cement, were so large that, according to their discoverer, Arthur Evans, members of his archeological crew "spent whole days in them without inconvenience." Curiously, the palace's many bathing rooms were apparently not linked to the drainage system. Water used for washing was fetched in containers by servants; then when the bather was through it was sponged up and carried out again.

The queen's bathroom at Knossos, as sketched by an artist at the dig, was a small alabaster-lined room decorated with frescoes. The terra-cotta bathtub was found outside the chamber and restored to its proper place. Anyone wanting a bath entered from the left, past a low wall and around a pillar.

would have disappeared. It would have looked very much like the other palaces, almost all of whose ruins rise only a single story or only part of a story aboveground. Visitors to the other sites get an excellent idea of what the storage rooms on the ground floor were like, but no idea whatsoever of the far grander and more interesting state rooms and apartments that were in the upper stories and are now vanished into the fragrant Minoan air.

Thanks to Evans, such a visualization is possible in parts of the Knossos palace, and it is profoundly interesting. Most impressive is a grand staircase that Evans found reasonably intact because it had been filled solid with rubble from the great holocaust that destroyed the palace for the second and last time. The staircase wound up to private and state apartments from the level of the main court, and also downward to other rooms below. Evans, digging straight into the side of a slope covering the palace ruin, hit this staircase in the middle, and was faced with the problem of preserving something that went both upward and downward from his point of entry. Working with great care, putting in structural members as he went, he was able to preserve the "down" part and reconstruct part of the "up" part.

The staircase was built around a light well that was open to the sky above, a necessary feature in Minoan architecture, since much of the interior space in the huge maze of a palace was windowless, depending for its light on what came down through an opening in the ceiling, or what shone in from rooms on the perimeter that did have windows.

What else does the palace at Knossos reveal? Royal apartments, for one thing, leading off from the grand staircase. They consist of suites of interconnected rooms—larger ones for socializing, smaller ones for sleeping, storage and bathing. There were even toilets, evidence of which is preserved in traces of seats over large drains that lead outside the palace. Wastes were flushed away by pouring water down an elaborate system of drains that included clay pipes carefully fitted together in sections and stone troughs to carry off rain water. The bathtubs, however, did not connect with the pipes. They were large comfortable affairs of glazed clay, often brightly decorated with pictures of fish and dolphins. Plugless, they apparently were bailed or sponged out by a servant when the bather was through washing, the dirty water thrown down the nearest drain.

There is a great swing in seasonal temperatures in Crete. Summers are stifling, but it can get uncomfortably raw in winter. By incorporating many open courts and light wells in the palace designs, plus colonnades, windows and connecting doorways for cross-drafts, Minoan architects solved the problem of making palace life tolerable in hot weather. The living rooms were large and airy. Some had interior rows of columns, suggesting that partitions may have been erected in winter, thus shrinking the space in a given room so that it could more easily be warmed by portable braziers.

Public or court business apparently was conducted in even larger rooms in the upper levels of the palace at Knossos, which raises the question of what to make of the so-called throne room, lying at a lower level. The throne room is a rather dark place with a low ceiling, its walls covered with frescoes of griffins —prone lions with the heads of birds. Evans gave the room its name because it did contain a handsome stone throne with a high curved back. It is there now,

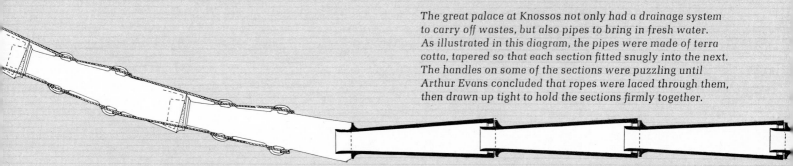

The great palace at Knossos not only had a drainage system to carry off wastes, but also pipes to bring in fresh water. As illustrated in this diagram, the pipes were made of terra cotta, tapered so that each section fitted snugly into the next. The handles on some of the sections were puzzling until Arthur Evans concluded that ropes were laced through them, then drawn up tight to hold the sections firmly together.

the "oldest throne in Europe," its seat gently hollowed for the comfort of the dignitary who sat on it.

Directly opposite the throne is a lustral chamber, a plastered area separated from the main room by a bench and a row of columns, its floor a few steps below that of the main room. There are several lustral chambers in the palace, including at least one tucked away in the royal apartments.

Evans gave them their name because he thought they were holy places in which some kind of ritual cleansing or bathing was undertaken in preparation for religious ceremonies. Other scholars have been highly skeptical of the theory; they think the sunken areas were just luxurious bathrooms. However, the presence of a lustral chamber inside the throne room, its sunken bathlike area located directly opposite the throne, does suggest that the priest-king conducted certain rites here. The German archeologist Helga Reusch offers an interesting alternative possibility that the throne was not a king's seat at all but that of the high priestess.

There is no mystery about the storerooms at Knossos. They were extensive, are well preserved and, in the palace's heyday, were crammed with wealth. There are archeological traces pointing to considerable hoards of gold. But nothing on the order of the treasure found by Schliemann at Mycenae has turned up at Knossos. The most impressive evidence of the palace's wealth comes in the form of huge storage jars for olive oil, perhaps as many as 400 of them, of which dozens were still intact in the ruins when Evans dug them out.

These jars were sensibly stored at ground level. An upper floor would have had to be extremely strong to carry all their weight—at least 470,000 pounds

when all 400 were full. Storing them in cellars below ground would have been equally impractical; hoisting them up and down, at half a ton or more per loaded jar, was clearly out of the question.

Altogether the oil-storage capacity at Knossos was about 62,000 gallons—a huge figure for that ancient time, and eloquent testimony to the great wealth of Crete, to the power of the central redistributive system that managed it and finally to the almost certain existence of a dense population on the island.

Only a very large and productive base could have made possible the building of such massive piles as the Minoan palaces, let alone maintaining them in splendid style for centuries. Evans estimated the population of Knossos in its heyday at 80,000 people for the palace and its surrounding town. Later estimates cut that figure in half, but even 40,000 is an impressive number. Add to it the people required to maintain the other palaces and all the large estates scattered over the island, and the true dimensions of the palace system in full bloom begin to emerge.

Minoan Crete was a fabulous place—busy, creative, unique. It supported a glittering upper class whose vices and cruelties—whatever they were—have vanished in the dust of centuries. Persisting are the glimpses of beauty, of great taste, of sophistication and a love of pleasure enjoyed by a people at their prime. Minos, if there was a Minos, ruled serene. Then, with a crash, the whole thing came down.

The second Minoan catastrophe in about 1450 B.C. is much more puzzling than the first. To begin with, the destruction of the palaces did not necessarily take place all at the same time—which makes an earthquake unlikely as the cause. Secondly, there is far greater evidence of fire; the palaces were not so much shaken down as incinerated, burning with a fierceness that has left some of their stones blackened even today. That stone and plaster edifices would burn at all can be explained by the great amount of wood used in their construction (partly for supporting members, partly for interior decoration) and by the great amounts of oil stored inside them. Finally, and most peculiar of all, is that the palaces, once gutted, were never rebuilt. With its religious and administrative centers gone, with the stopping of the redistributive heart that kept the social blood flowing, Minoan palace society apparently collapsed.

Any number of theories have been advanced to explain that dramatic collapse. They fall into three categories—or into combinations of the three: (1) natural catastrophe, such as earthquake, (2) foreign invasion and (3) domestic upheaval.

Interesting arguments can be made for each explanation, but until very recently none has been able to stand up satisfactorily under the growing amount of information that archeologists in the Aegean continue to produce. In 1939 the late Spyridon Marinatos, who would later become Inspector General of Antiquities for all Greece, suggested that the fall of Minoan culture was connected to a huge volcanic explosion that had taken place on the island of Thera (modern Santorini) 70 miles away. His idea, crudely stated, was that Crete had literally been knocked flat in some way by that cataclysmic event.

The comments that greeted Marinatos' suggestion were on the order of: "provocative," "suggestive," "highly original," "worth exploring." But they all boiled down to: "We don't know nearly enough about what happened on Thera to begin to know its effect on Crete. There should be a lot more investigation done on this subject."

In recent years a great deal of investigation has been done and knowledge is pouring in. It now appears that the fates of Thera and Crete were indeed linked, although the exact nature of the linkage is tricky to establish. Nevertheless, a new hypothesis is emerging that satisfies most of the contradictions that have plagued previous hypotheses. Furthermore, it sits comfortably with some of the ideas basic to Colin Renfrew's multiplier effect.

Vestiges of the Great Minoan Royal Palaces

The symbolic U-shaped horns of consecration loom over a part of the palace at Knossos, reconstructed by archeologist Arthur Evans.

Although Crete is well sprinkled with the remains of Minoan villages, luxurious country estates and even some sizable towns, so far only five sites have been found that can truly be described as palatial. These fantastic royal residences are unmistakable—with their mazes of private apartments, public reception halls, endless cubicles, corridors and storage facilities, all built around a courtyard. Although the five palaces differ wide-ly from one another in detail, they have these same basic features. All except one *(pages 88-89)* were the economic and political nuclei of their respective domains.

Knossos was the first of the great Cretan ruins to be recognized as a palace—and was so identified in 1900 by Arthur Evans. Almost immediately three more were discovered. But since then, only one—Kato Zakro in 1961 —has been added to the list, although archeologists have been assiduously combing the Cretan countryside for traces of others. It now begins to look as if five may be the final total—which is curious, because all five are located in the eastern half of Crete, despite the fact that the larger western area contained its share of towns, shrines and a fairly dense population. Who governed those western settlements and from where are questions that have gone unanswered.

Mallia: Facing the Cyclades

The existence of a promising Minoan ruin on the seacoast east of Knossos was suspected from the end of the last century when a shepherd picked up some gold objects there. Archeologists moved in and in 1915 found a palace —Mallia—located at the center of a town that covered a square kilometer.

Work on the palace had started about 2000 B.C. and continued for more than 500 years. Its closeness to the water made it a thriving seaport—and also may have led to its destruction in 1450 B.C. Of all the Mi-noan palaces that were wrecked at the time, Mallia was the most directly exposed to the great tidal waves set in motion by the eruption at Thera. Its Minoan name is unknown. It was called Mallia by the Greeks, from their word *omalion*, which means flat.

A limestone wheel measuring three feet across and with indentations around its edge was found embedded in the floor of an arcade next to Mallia's main court. Experts cannot decide if it was used to play a game or in a religious ritual.

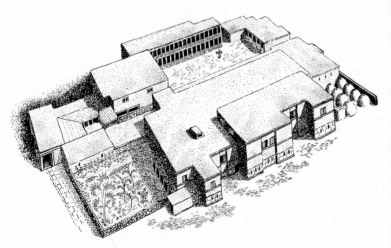

An aerial drawing of the palace at Mallia is based on studies by art historian J. W. Graham. The main court is at the rear in this rendering. The royal apartments and public rooms are situated at the front, and the main palace entrance is at left.

Mallia today retains only the lower parts of its ground-floor paving stones and walls. Two storage jars as tall as men —called pithoi—stand in the ruin; on the nearest one can be seen the surface decorations designed to simulate the ropes employed to move these enormously heavy terra-cotta vessels. Snow-capped Mount Dikte rises in the background; before it spreads the rich farming plain that contributed so much to Mallia's emergence as an important palace center.

Kato Zakro: Commanding the Eastern Mediterranean

Kato Zakro lies at the extreme eastern tip of Crete, walled off from the rest of the island by high mountains. With its fine bay it was an important naval base and a busy commercial port from which trading ships went regularly to Egypt and Palestine.

Kato Zakro fell in a single, violent instant that left the palace a smoking ruin. Its inhabitants fled—and never went back. As a result, excavators of the site have found things there in an abundance that no other palace has provided: tools, such raw materials as wood and metals, household objects, kitchen equipment, bits of food—all scattered wildly and untouched since the day of destruction. For a long time after its demolition the site apparently was regarded as a holy place and sedulously avoided.

A cistern was located on the east side of the palace, handy
to the royal apartments. Fed by a spring that still flows, the
well has excellently preserved stone steps leading to it.

Although Kato Zakro, like all Minoan palaces, had its fertile
plain, the main focus of its people was toward the sea. The
edifice was built on a grade that descended to a central court
(far left). The ruins in the foreground are the remnants
of what were once storerooms and workshops. The royal
apartments and the public rooms were located off to the left.

Phaistos: Queen of the South Coast

Second only to Knossos in size and wealth, the palace of Phaistos, on Crete's south coast, is, in its way, the finest on the island. It is better situated than Knossos, located on a rise of ground with an unsurpassed view across a green valley to blue mountains beyond. The main entrance to Phaistos was superior to that at Knossos, consisting of an impressive flight of stone steps 45 feet wide. Phaistos is also better preserved, but to the excavator presents similar problems. It was destroyed twice by earthquake —and rebuilt each time—then finally sacked and burned by attackers in 1450 B.C. Unlike Knossos, whose royal apartments were along the side of the central court, those at Phaistos were at the end, each one with its own private, colonnaded garden.

Phaistos' central court was long and narrow and, like all the others, stone paved. This view of its north end looks past the royal suite at right toward Crete's highest mountain: Ida.

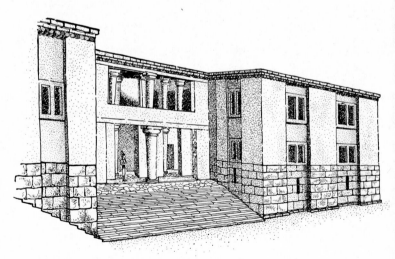

A rendering of the palace's west façade was made by J. W. Graham. The main entrance was up a broad flight of steps to a large double doorway bisected by a column that tapered gradually toward the base—a design favored by the Minoans.

To set off the palace entrance properly, its architects provided a spacious west courtyard (foreground). From there, one proceeded up a shallow flight of 12 stone steps, all of them built with a very slight downward slope so that rain water would run off the stairs rather than lie in puddles.

Hagia Triada: A Vest-Pocket Marvel

A mini-palace or a supervilla? Arguments go on about the true identity of this most charming of all Minoan ruins, known by its modern Greek name Hagia Triada, meaning Holy Trinity. It is only a mile or so away from the palace at Phaistos, over a small hill, and it commands a stunning view of the sea and Mount Ida. Since true palaces could not reasonably have existed side by side, scholars strongly suspect that Hagia Triada was a summer residence for the rulers at Phaistos. This possibility was strengthened by the discovery of a road that connected the two and by the quality of workmanship at Hagia Triada, with its alabaster-faced walls and lavish frescoes. It is a sumptuous place, with intimate dimensions, making Phaistos seem cold and bare by contrast.

The many staircases at Hagia Triada, like this narrow flight, were built of superbly cut stones, which are in excellent condition even today. These steps descend from the central court level to an area devoted to workshops and storerooms.

Hagia Triada is built on an L-shaped plan, cunningly designed so that its rooms cascade down a gentle slope, its suites of chambers connected to one another by numerous flights of steps. The palace entrance was at the top of the incline at left, the royal apartments in the foreground. The main court was at center. Workshops were located at the right. Many valuables have been found here: gold jewelry and exquisitely carved steatite jars—all attesting to royal occupancy.

Chapter Four: Lost Atlantis

About 590 B.C. a distinguished Athenian citizen paid a visit to Egypt. He was the statesman Solon, who had just finished codifying a new set of laws for the Athenians and was now traveling, prudently absenting himself from Athens while his fractious fellow citizens digested the stiff new laws he had just stuffed down their throats.

While in Egypt, Solon talked to several learned priest-historians who impressed him mightily with their great knowledge of the past. Greek history was a muddle of myths handed down, from no one knew exactly where, to a people who had learned to read and write only in the previous hundred years or so. By contrast, Egyptian history was neatly chronicled on papyrus and stone, and wound back for a couple of thousand years. Solon listened intently to what he was told, hoping to learn something about the prehistory of his own people. One story he brought back was unforgettable. It described an island empire —large, powerful, highly civilized—that in a single day of dire catastrophe had sunk into the sea and disappeared forever.

Through Solon's descendants, one of them a cousin of the philosopher Plato, the story was preserved. Ultimately Plato wrote it down in his dialogues. The legend of Atlantis is believed to have worked its way into Western thought in this way.

Thera—once a single round island—has been crescent-shaped since its center fell into the sea about 1500 B.C., leaving 1,100-foot cliffs and two small islands edging a central lagoon (opposite). Thera's original contours are shown in light blue in the diagram at left. The islands in the middle of the lagoon are the tops of a still-active volcano.

Because Plato was so specific about the island's supposed size and location, seekers of a submerged Atlantis have usually looked for it in the Atlantic Ocean. They have had no success. Nor will they ever; modern knowledge of the ocean bottom, of continent formation and continental shelves, has ruled out any possibility that the Atlantic Ocean ever held a large populated island.

How, then, is the story of Atlantis, as reported by those Egyptian scholars, to be accounted for? Two modern investigators, Irish classicist J. V. Luce and Greek scientist A. G. Galanopoulos, have looked long and hard at this question. In their writings they have come up with essentially the same answer. They suggest that the proper way to approach the problem is to begin with Plato, to agree that Plato is to be taken seriously but not literally. In short, he *was* writing about something real, but his description of it—as to size, layout, population, age and government—was somewhat fanciful, created to serve a philosophical rather than a historical purpose.

Therefore, they say, do not look at the legend through Plato's eyes but through the eyes of the Egyptians. Look for the event *behind* the Platonic myth, some catastrophe that the Egyptians might have heard about, that could have caused them to get the Atlantis story started. That catastrophe might even have occurred close at hand in the Mediterranean—a likelihood that gained increasingly in strength as the two modern investigators conscientiously ran down every other possibility and concluded that there was no other place in the world that could have contained an Atlantis.

So, back to the view from Egypt. The Egyptians were essentially a land and river people. Throughout a long history they had looked north from the Nile Delta, out across the "great green," as they called the Mediterranean Sea, to a rich and somewhat mysterious island empire that lay below the horizon an unknown distance away. They knew this place only indirectly: through its people, who came southeast in their ships to trade with Egypt.

If this theory was right, the people of Atlantis were none other than the Keftiu, men from Crete. They probably brought lumber, olive oil, woven goods, pottery and bronze objects with them, and traded for papyrus, stoneware, copper and gold. But suddenly they stopped coming. At about the same time rumors began to drift south of a terrible catastrophe that had occurred, a shattering convulsion that had rent an island. It is conceivable that the Egyptians may have heard ponderous explosions drumming across the sky, may even have coughed and spat in a pall of dust that descended on them. These phenomena, coupled with the disappearance of the men from Crete,

could have suggested to the Egyptians that Crete itself had disappeared.

At any rate, a garbled account of some such island disaster survived in Egyptian records and was duly told to Solon nearly a thousand years later when he visited Egypt. Since no Greek of Solon's day had any inkling of the existence of a unique Cretan culture, he probably took the tale more imaginatively than it was intended. Either he or Plato gave the vanished island the name Atlantis, and it has stuck.

Crete, of course, had not vanished, but another island had—almost. This was Thera, southernmost of the Cyclades and only 70 miles from Crete. Thera was a roundish island about 10 or 12 miles across, the visible tip of a large volcano rising from the sea

floor of the Mediterranean, built up as the result of successive eruptions that had taken place in the remote past. During the Bronze Age, Thera may have looked something like an island Fujiyama or Vesuvius, with a fairly symmetrical cone, deeply scored by erosion, probably with a vent and a small crater at the top. Since volcanic soil is highly nourishing, Thera was undoubtedly green on its flatter lower slopes, given over to the vines and farms and groves of the large population now known to have lived on it. Only the steeper, higher slope of the upper cone —cinders or lava—would have remained bare.

Then Thera, for so long quiescent, erupted again, shooting up a great volume of rocks, cinders and ash. The new activity culminated in one or more tremendous explosions that were the result of intolerable gas and heat pressures building up from below faster than they could be relieved by the escape of material through a rather narrow vent—or throat—in the center of the cone. The bangs were truly epic, and when

The people of Thera, like all Aegean islanders of their day, got much of their living from the sea. In this scene of the busy harbor at Akrotiri, some women haggle over the purchase of fish; octopuses are spread out on a pole to dry; fishermen work on their nets; and men are unloading the cargo from a newly arrived ship. The Therans had an exceptionally well-organized export trade, mostly in oil from olive groves on their own island. Much of the Theran oil went to Crete in exchange for fine pottery and other luxury goods. But all Thera's thriving activities came to an abrupt end in 1500 B.C. when the volcano, shown in the background, exploded.

the last one went off, spewing out millions and millions of tons of material, there was left a huge, empty undersea space, where all the gas and ejecta had come from. The entire mountain fell into this hole and disappeared under the water.

What once had been a round island was now a crescent, with a couple of smaller bits left sticking out of the water around the edges of the hole. What had once been a 5,000-foot peak was now a lagoon seven miles across, surrounded with a lunar landscape of steep lava cliffs plunging a thousand feet to the sea and dropping below the surface a thousand feet more. The lagoon was, in fact, an immense crater, deeper than the surrounding sea. On top of what was left of the island—when all the dust and smoke had cleared away—sat a mantle of newly deposited ash, in some places up to 200 feet thick.

Exactly when did this happen? When the late Greek archeologist Spyridon Marinatos first cocked an inquiring eye at this strange shattered island back in 1932, no one was quite sure. Marinatos himself was interested because of another sticky problem he was beginning to wrestle with: What had knocked down all the palaces on Crete? Specifically, what had wrenched out of place some very heavy stone blocks

at a ruin next to the water at Amnisos, a port of Knossos, on Crete's north coast? Marinatos chewed over this problem for seven years, then published a daring article suggesting that the Theran eruption had destroyed Minoan civilization.

To make this radical proposal acceptable, experts had to find answers to two questions. First was the question of force: Could the explosion on Thera really have been destructive enough to flatten Crete, whose nearest point was a good 70 miles distant? Second was the question of timing: Did the explosion occur at the same time the palaces on Crete fell, or at some other time entirely?

For the first question there existed a handy modern model: a similar volcanic explosion had occurred in 1883 at Krakatoa in the Sunda Strait between Sumatra and Java. The circumstances at Krakatoa have remarkable parallels with those at Thera. Krakatoa, too, was a small island with a long history of volcanism, climaxing in the same kind of frightful burst,

At a corner in one of Akrotiri's typically narrow streets, neighbors chat outside the entrance to a house. Studies of the harbor town's ruins have revealed that many houses were built of massive stone blocks and had doorways supported by posts and lintels made of wood. In this scene, a farmer leads a donkey laden with pots of olive oil and a basket of produce.

accompanied by a huge outpouring of ash and ending with a similar collapse and disappearance into the sea of a large part of the island.

The value of Krakatoa as a model was that its eruption was well documented. A great deal about it had been recorded by observers living in the area and by ships passing through at the time. There is no question about the destructiveness. In the neighborhood of the Sunda Strait alone, 300 villages were swamped and 36,000 people killed. Seismic sea waves on nearby coasts reached a height of 130 feet. The blast cracked masonry buildings a hundred miles away. The air stank with noxious gases. Chunks of rock and pumice were flung over a wide area. Three days later ash and dust were still falling in large quantities on the decks of ships 1,600 miles away. The finest dust took many months to settle, treating people in all parts of the world to some of the most beautiful sunsets they would ever see.

For several years before it gave any evidence that it might erupt, Krakatoa had been acting up with a series of increasingly violent earthquakes that were felt throughout the region. Then volcanic activity began, growing in intensity over a period of three months. The climax came with four extraordinarily loud detonations clearly heard by many people in Australia, 2,000 miles to the southeast, and reportedly heard on Rodrigues Island, 3,000 miles to the west. Locally —within a couple of hundred miles—the explosions were deafening. For several months after the climax, ships in the Indian Ocean found themselves plowing through large rafts of floating pumice.

Can Krakatoa be compared to Thera? Definitely yes, in the sense that the same general series of events occurred in both places.

The Theran catastrophe was considerably larger than the Krakatoan; Thera's crater was four or five times as big and the amount of material it ejected correspondingly greater. But that does not necessarily mean it was four or five times as destructive. The critical consideration is the force of the climactic explosions. A large firecracker fizzling away its power in a slow flash that takes half a second has nothing like the force of a little firecracker that goes off almost instantaneously. Exploding firecrackers and exploding volcanoes are alike in that both represent rapid build-ups of pressure within enclosed spaces. The size of the bang that results is measured not only by the amount of powder inside but also by the amount of pressure required to burst open the casing and by the suddenness with which the bursting takes place.

Some highly sophisticated studies of Thera have been made in recent years by volcanologists, and a great deal learned about it. Most agree that the event on Thera was extremely large, and theoretically capable of inflicting great damage on Crete. That it actually did so, however, has not been conclusively established. The damage could have come from earthquakes associated with or coinciding with the Theran eruption, or from direct blast. But most attention has been focused on two other phenomena: ash-fall and tsunamis (seismic sea waves). Both are considered better candidates for explaining the Cretan disaster.

"Tsunami" derives from the Japanese word for harbor wave. It is an appropriate word. In their narrow harbors and inland seas the Japanese throughout their history have had bitter experience with tsunamis. They are caused by the movement of large volumes of earth substance—the result of an earthquake on

the ocean bottom or the volcanic collapse of an island. Either is capable of sending a tremor out through the surrounding water like the ripple that travels across a pool when a stone is dropped in it, but on a vastly greater scale.

Tsunamis move at speeds of up to 400 miles per hour, depending on the depth of the sea bottom. Racing over the open ocean, they are very broad but very low: a hundred miles or more wide but only a few feet high. A ship at sea—encountering a wave so wide, so low and traveling so fast—probably will not notice it at all. But as that giant ripple reaches an obstruction—an island or a coast—and as the depth becomes increasingly shallow, bottom-drag causes the wave to crest higher and higher until it may reach a height of several hundred feet. This immense wall of water will flood a shore—going higher yet if constricted in a long, narrow, funnel-like bay—arriving totally without warning and drowning the entire area in a matter of minutes. The wave is equally damaging when it recedes; the backwash goes out in a roaring torrent, sucking everything along with it.

Marinatos had tsunamis in mind when he was inspecting those wrenched building blocks on the Cretan coast near Knossos. He thought of tsunamis again when, far above sea level on the Cycladic island of Anaphe, he found bits of pumice: light spongelike lava ejecta that had ridden a great wave and apparently were left behind to mark the high point of the wave's upreach.

The argument for damage by ash-fall is equally impressive. It has been calculated that an outburst on the scale of Thera could have smothered eastern Crete with a blanket of ash several inches thick. This load would have been enough to destroy crops and

Two women spinning wool gather with their neighbors in a small Theran square to admire a monkey brought from Egypt by a trader.

In the olive groves planted on the hillsides overlooking Akrotiri, boys tend mixed flocks of sheep and goats; the town itself, at far left, sits serenely on the edge of the sea.

put fields out of business for several years. A layer as much as three feet deep would have destroyed trees and knocked down buildings.

Calculations of this sort were fine for the ash enthusiasts, except for the awkward fact that there did not seem to be any ash on Crete. Investigators digging in the palace sites early in the 20th Century had no idea that ash-fall might be connected with destruction, and consequently did not look about for it. In any event they would have had difficulty finding it. Volcanic ash tends to disintegrate to dust and get mixed with the surrounding soil. For this reason later investigators, although looking for ash, also were unable to find any. After many centuries of plowing, digging, water erosion and being blown about by the wind, ash either washes into the sea, disappears entirely or is no longer recognizable as ash except under the microscope, where its tiny glassy particles can be detected—by experts—in a mixture of other soil materials. As a result of this difficulty in recognizing ash, some experienced archeologists as recently as 1973 were still maintaining that there was none on Crete, and that an explanation for the Minoan collapse would have to be found elsewhere.

All this in the face of some interesting evidence that was beginning to appear from the bottom of the sea. Since 1947 oceanographic vessels have been extracting cores—long, tubular borings of sea-bottom material—from the eastern Mediterranean and have been analyzing the different layers that have accumulated there. Sea-bottom cores provide good clues to events on land, since it is very quiet down there compared to the turbulent environment up above the surface. When anything—ash, fish bones, small shelled creatures—sinks to the bottom, it is gradually covered by layers of other material filtering down and is safely locked in place. A core can tell a great deal about what happened thousands, and in some cases millions, of years ago.

The cores from the eastern Mediterranean contain ash. It is thickest in the samples collected closest to Thera, indicating that their source was that island. Some miles away the ash layers grow thinner. Finally, at great distances from Thera, they peter out entirely. As it turns out, there are two distinct ash layers in the cores. Clearly there had been two great volcanic outbursts widely separated in time. The problem was to find out if either eruption was the one that might have affected the Minoan palaces.

There is an elegant solution to this problem. Ash

A woman of Akrotiri employs a clay rack to grill shish kebab.

consists of small fragments of volcanic ejecta. As lava comes rushing up the throat of a volcano, its gases expand rapidly, under certain conditions turning the ejecta into a kind of stony foam full of tiny air holes. This is pumice. Though pumice looks like rock, it is actually a kind of volcanic glass. It may come hurtling up in large chunks or in small bits, depending on how badly it is jostled about during its ejection. Most pumice ranges downward from pebble size to the finest dust. That small stuff is normally called tephra; and tephra is what covers Thera and is also found in layers in the surrounding sea bottom.

Since conditions beneath the surface of the earth vary from volcano to volcano, what is discharged at different times or at different places is never exactly the same. Variations can be determined in the laboratory with great precision by measuring the angle at which light bounces off the tephra samples. Each has a so-called refractive index, and each is unique. The huge pile of tephra that lies on Thera today has an index of 1.509. So does all the tephra strewn about on the sea bottom. The lower older layer of tephra in the cores from the sea bottom has an index of 1.521. It traces to an eruption that took place about 25,000 years ago and does not concern us here except to note how neatly one can identify a particular event.

Cores clearly map the distribution of Theran tephra on the sea bottom. It spreads downwind, mainly in a southeasterly direction, over an area of about 120,000 square miles. This pattern includes the eastern half of Crete, indicating that there must have been a generous ash-fall there, despite the past failure of archeologists to find any. In 1971 two American volcanologists, Dorothy and Charles Vitaliano, studied the soil in a number of sites on Crete and came away with several samples of 1.509 tephra, proving conclusively that ash from the big Theran blast had fallen there. Its rarity today is explained by the perishability of the glass itself.

So, tsunamis may have damaged Crete. Ash-fall may have done so. But to prove either theory, it is necessary to deal with the second of the two problems already mentioned: the problem of timing. In short, when did Thera blow its top, and when did the Minoan palaces fall? For one to have caused the other directly, it is necessary—and not easy—to demonstrate that they happened at the same time.

Geological studies of the tephra layers on Thera could say a great deal about the nature of the eruption, but not when it happened. The best available evidence on timing was from some preliminary 19th Century excavations on Thera, which had produced pottery that could be crudely dated within a hundred years or so of 1500 B.C. Better evidence, col-

Akrotiri had its metalworking shops, and metal vessels like the three below have been found in the ash. The shallow utensil is called a frying pan because of its shape; its true use is not known. Another find was a saddle-shaped anvil (right); presumably the smith straddled one end while he used the other to bang a vessel into shape with a stone hammer. The worker in the foreground is riveting a handle to a bronze pot.

lected under controlled conditions in a modern excavation, was needed.

Reenter Professor Marinatos. Determined to find evidence of Minoan occupancy on Thera itself, spurred by those earlier finds of pottery, and particularly by reports of buried houses and more pottery at a site called Akrotiri near the southern tip of the crescent-shaped main island, he chose the latter as a likely spot to begin digging. A powerful practical consideration also dictated this choice. The blanket of ash that covers Thera is generally so deep that clearing off this overburden is a hopeless task for an archeologist. But there has been a great deal of surface erosion in certain parts of Thera. One of the principal attractions of Akrotiri was that the tephra there was only a few feet thick in some places.

Marinatos started digging in 1967. His finds, before he was killed in a fall at the site in 1974, were truly miraculous. They led him deeper and deeper into the tephra layer as he literally mined out—room after room, street after street—the collapsed remains of a large Cycladic-Minoan town. Marinatos did not know what part of it he had discovered, whether he was working near its center or on the outskirts. He did suspect that it stretched along the coast for some distance to include a part of the island that is now sunk beneath the sea. He thought that as many as 30,000 people may have been living in this part of Thera when the catastrophe occurred.

More important than size is the quality and condition of the town that Marinatos found. Unlike any other known Minoan site, Akrotiri is exactly the way it was on the day disaster hit it. Tephra is an even better preservative than ocean sediment. Chemically

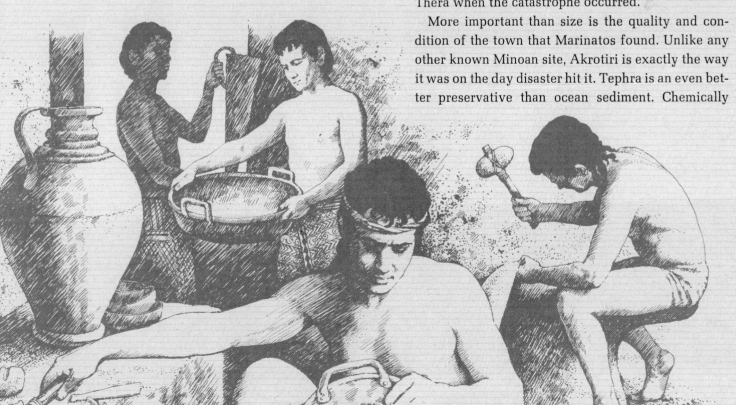

almost neutral, it has acted like a heavy packing —almost like snow—filtering into every cranny, collapsing roofs as its weight got too heavy, buckling staircases, crushing pottery, but gradually filling in everything and holding it just so ever since.

Akrotiri is an extraordinary place, both for what it has and for what it has not. It has already yielded at least half a dozen of the most beautiful and certainly the most complete Minoan frescoes ever found (pages 111-119). But it has not yielded a palace. Marinatos did not know where to look for one. He was not even sure that one existed, although on the model of the archeological sites on Crete, it seems highly likely that somewhere on Thera there was a palace.

Stranger yet, there are next to no skeletons in this dusty mausoleum. Nor is there any treasure. The impression one gets, trudging through the narrow streets that have been excavated in the dig, pausing in a small town square, peering into doorways and windows, is of a town abandoned, powdered every-

where with dust. Here was no Pompeii where people were surprised and caught by the sudden eruption of a Vesuvius: men overtaken while sprinting through the streets, calcified dogs writhing in their final agony, beans on the stove. Everything easily movable at Akrotiri—everything of value—is gone, along with all the people. What remains—besides those gorgeous frescoes, which, of course, could not be removed—are pots, a great many of them. Most of these were either cheap ones not considered worth taking by frantic, overburdened householders, or big heavy ones, too big to be moved in a hurry. Akrotiri, it is plain, was cleaned out in great haste and abandoned.

During the years he worked on the site, Marinatos developed some pretty clear ideas about what happened there. From examination of some of the tumbled-down walls he came to the conclusion that the eruption had been preceded by a series of earthquakes (presumably like those known to have preceded the Krakatoa blast). He found evidence that

Alerted by premonitory earthquakes that damaged their homes, and now terrified by the choking fumes spewing from the active volcano above their town, the inhabitants of Akrotiri prepare to flee. They have gathered their most valuable and most easily portable possessions—jewelry, textiles and fine pottery—and are now headed for the waterfront, where a fleet of vessels will carry them away from the holocaust. The question of where they went—to Crete, or west to other Cycladic islands, or on to the Greek mainland—remains unanswered. Archeologists are only certain that the evacuation of Akrotiri was sudden—and apparently successful. No human remains have been found.

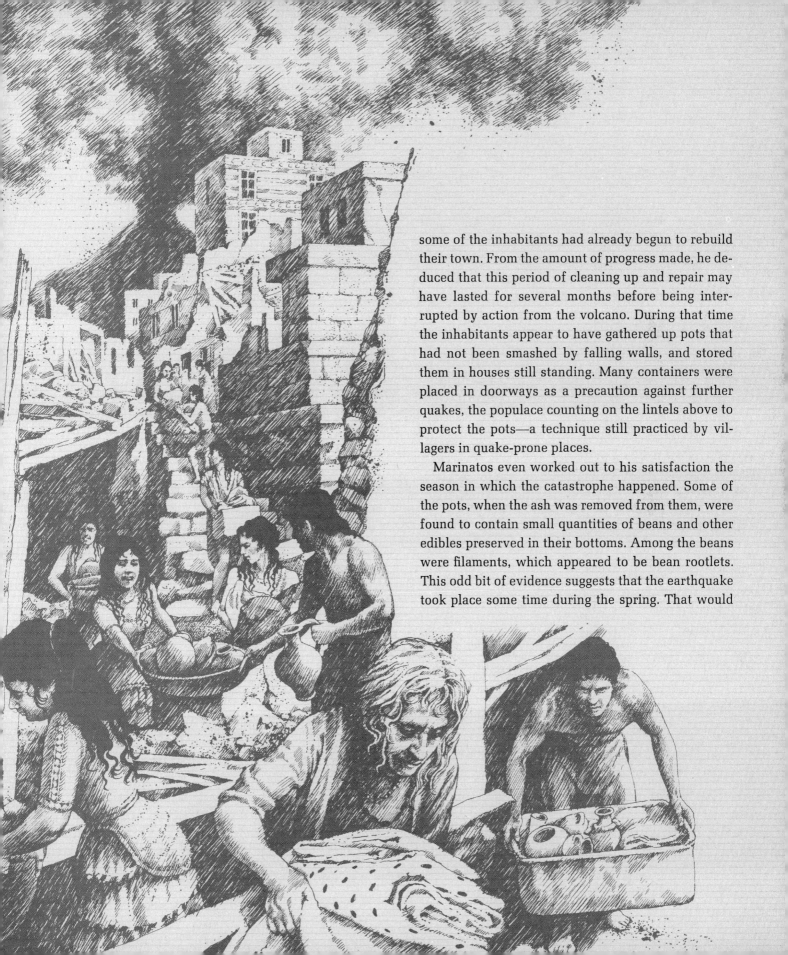

some of the inhabitants had already begun to rebuild their town. From the amount of progress made, he deduced that this period of cleaning up and repair may have lasted for several months before being interrupted by action from the volcano. During that time the inhabitants appear to have gathered up pots that had not been smashed by falling walls, and stored them in houses still standing. Many containers were placed in doorways as a precaution against further quakes, the populace counting on the lintels above to protect the pots—a technique still practiced by villagers in quake-prone places.

Marinatos even worked out to his satisfaction the season in which the catastrophe happened. Some of the pots, when the ash was removed from them, were found to contain small quantities of beans and other edibles preserved in their bottoms. Among the beans were filaments, which appeared to be bean rootlets. This odd bit of evidence suggests that the earthquake took place some time during the spring. That would explain the near emptiness of the pots: the preceding fall's stores would have been eaten by people digging themselves out and trying to get their lives together after the quakes. The onset of volcanic activity would have occurred during the late summer or early fall; the beans in the pots would have remained there all through the summer—long enough to sprout but not long enough for the pots to have been filled by the next season's crop. A summer eruption is confirmed by the pattern of ash-fall in the sea, as shown by the sea-bottom cores. The fall is almost all to the southeast of Thera, indicating that the ash had been blown in that direction by the northerly winds that prevail there in summer.

Leaving, for a moment, the archeological clues provided by Akrotiri, one can go back to Thera's quarry and confirm Marinatos' ideas rather well by looking at the layers of ash-fall that have been laid open, right down to bedrock. Here the evidence is of a different sort, but very clear. Whatever warnings the volcano may have given the inhabitants, its first eruptive act was a great spout of rather coarse pumice —gray in color but with a reddish-brown tint to it. It can be assumed that when this horrible dry rain began to descend, the inhabitants of Thera gathered up their valuables and fled the island by boat. The blast may have lasted a few hours, a few days or even a few weeks. Before the eruption was through, it deposited a layer of pumice on the island nearly 15 feet thick. Following this the volcano emitted a few feeble hiccups (detectable in five different layers of ash atop the pumice, none of them more than a few inches thick) before letting go with its final act, a cough of truly cosmic dimensions that deposited a crushing load of fine white ash. That is what cov-

ers Thera today. In some places it runs 200 feet deep.

Volcanologists, studying those layers and noticing signs of weather erosion between them, first concluded that the eruption had taken place over a number of years. Now, understanding better the erosional characteristics of tephra and noting that there is absolutely no accumulation of topsoil between any of the layers, they believe that the entire volcanic cycle —from first pumice blast to final collapse and disappearance of the mountain—must be classed as a single event. It could have been compressed into a few days or weeks, and certainly would not have taken longer than a few months. This timetable satisfies Marinatos' archeological conclusion, and it also matches the behavior of the Krakatoa model.

Akrotiri today is a maze of steel supports holding up a corrugated shed roof that completely covers the dig. It extends over an acre and a half, and continues to grow. A fascinating haul has come from it: products of the local pottery industry, fine pottery imported from Crete in the various styles fashionable at the time, details of house construction (in which a great deal of wood was apparently used in the upper stories), metal household vessels, even a bed. Not the bed itself, but the ghost of a bed. The wood that made it, the hide that covered it and the ropes that laced it have all disintegrated, but the space that those materials once occupied in the ash that solidly filled the bedroom remains. A bed-shaped space. It has been carefully filled with plaster of Paris, and a Theran bed emerges (page 109). A duplicate of that plaster model, made of the proper materials, now stands in the National Archeological Museum of Athens. Of all the things that beckon from Akrotiri, that bed

Text continued on page 107

Akrotiri: A City Preserved in Volcanic Ash

Hidden beneath a protective blanket of volcanic ash for more than three millennia, Akrotiri, a large port on Thera, is coming to light again. Archeologist Spyridon Marinatos began the excavations there in 1967; when he died in 1974 he had already exposed more than an acre of the town's ruins. Much still awaits excavation and analysis. Many questions remain. How big was it? Did it have a palace? But the work already done has proven extraordinarily interesting.

No human skeletons have been discovered in Akrotiri, nor any treasure. From their absence it can be assumed that the inhabitants had time to gather up their most valued possessions when the nearby volcano began to act up, and to flee before its catastrophic final explosion. But the people of Thera did leave a great deal behind: quantities of everyday utensils, some breathtaking frescoes (pages 111-119) and—most revealing—the buildings they lived and worked in.

Doorframes at Akrotiri have been reconstructed with great fidelity by pouring concrete into the empty spaces left in the compacted ash by the disintegrated original wooden posts and lintels. This view from a street looks through a room in one house, across a small town square, to the doors and windows of another house.

The center of the excavation at Akrotiri consists of a large complex of rooms that were part of a compound of connected houses. The ruins at the far right, near the diggers' catwalk, actually comprise the second stories of buildings; the lower levels will be unearthed only after the upper ones have been studied and shored up. The opening at the center of the photograph, with a sign propped up beside it, leads to the room that originally contained the famous Spring Fresco (page 118).

A flight of stone steps was crushed by the weight of ash-fall. But the ash was also a boon to archeologists: sifting in everywhere, it often held up walls and cushioned artifacts.

A patch of newly unearthed fresco (foreground) contains the sterns of two passing ships. The level above the fresco appears to be a bathroom decorated with a band of tinted plaster.

Discovered in one room—possibly a kitchen—were several dozen large pots and small vessels. Except for the removal of ash, they were left as found for analysis of their contents: some held food particles, others remnants of an unidentified white substance.

beckons one closest. It is easy to imagine oneself in it —lying there, then leaping up at the appalling roar of erupting pumice, sweeping one's small valuables into a sack and running for the beach.

Less poignant than the bed, but far more important archeologically, is the huge array of pots already collected. A massive effort to sort them out and classify them has given a very clear picture of the range of styles in use at the time of the catastrophe. And that picture, by its very clarity, raises the last and perhaps the most perplexing question of all in dealing with the relationship between the Theran explosion and the fall of the palaces on Crete.

A glance at the pottery sequence on page 35 will show that a particularly beautiful and distinctive style—based on pictures of shells, seaweed, fish and other underwater motifs, and known as the Marine style—flourished on Crete for 50 years, between 1500 and 1450 B.C. Those dates must be regarded as pretty accurate. Evidence from many directions and intensive study by many experts following in Arthur Evans' footsteps anchor them. They do not budge easily. Nor does the date of the eruption—1500 B.C.—budge much. But why should they budge at all?

Because at Akrotiri there is no late Marine style pottery from Crete. That curious fact is the key to the situation. The last pot imported to Thera from Crete may have arrived the day of the eruption. Thereafter the door was sealed, nothing more came. On that same day—or weeks or months later, depending on how long the eruption on Thera lasted —tsunamis would have battered the Cretan coast and ash would have choked it. According to those who believe that the eruption on Thera was directly responsible for the fall of the palaces on Crete, those palaces would have collapsed at the very same time.

But if they did crash, how does one account for the emergence on Crete 50 years later of the late, or mature, Marine style of pottery?

One cannot. Those 50 years do not compress neatly into one date. For all the seductiveness of the blast-ash-tsunami-collapse theory, it does not hold up. The best recent studies of the Minoan palaces makes it clear that they did not all go down in 1500 B.C. They appear to have fallen at various times, most of them around 1450 B.C. One of them, Knossos, did not really fall at all. The damage there was nothing like that suffered at Mallia, Phaistos and Kato Zakro. In fact, no single volcanic cause—blast, tsunami, earthquake, ash-fall—or even a combination of them—can account satisfactorily for the destruction of all the palaces on Crete.

Mallia, being on the north coast and very near the water, may well have been destroyed by tsunamis. But why wasn't Knossos? Was it too far inland, too sheltered by surrounding hills? Not if one thinks of waves several hundred feet high. Very well, let us assume smaller tsunamis that would have spared Knossos; how, then, do we account for the fall of Phaistos, which was on the opposite side of Crete and might not have been seriously affected by tsunamis at all? Worse, how do we account for the destruction of the villas of the rich, scattered about the country, many of them out of the reach of any conceivable wave?

Blast?

If blast destroyed Mallia, how could it cross a high mountain range to destroy Phaistos; or Kato Zakro, hidden down behind a steep chasm, facing east, away from Thera, and totally protected?

That leaves ash—of all the potentially destructive agents from Thera the only one that could have distributed its influence fairly evenly over the entire eastern half of Crete. In other words, if a case can be made for ash as a contributor to the fall of any palace, that case should stand up equally well for the others. An awkward fact is that probably only a few inches of ash fell on Crete. However, even that small deposit would have been enough to destroy crops for several seasons—enough to produce a scenario of misfortune and collapse.

Ruined crops can cause starvation. Starvation can cause social unrest. Social unrest can cause the loosening of authority. These distractions can cause dislocations in the system that makes and distributes food and goods—which brings us back to where we came in: to the redistributive system, to Colin Renfrew's model, to the multiplier effect.

Microbiologist and ecologist René Dubos has observed that any unusually successful social innovation can be depended upon to be carried to the point of absurdity. The Minoan palace system was such an innovation. The ability of Minoan society to organize itself through a network of palace centers, to receive and distribute goods on a scale of efficiency not practiced elsewhere in the Aegean world, to conduct a large and successful overseas trade, protected presumably by a strong navy that also protected Crete itself—all these things brought Crete to a peak of opulence that we can even now get glimpses of in the palace ruins and in the villas of the wealthy that dotted the countryside.

But was the system ever "absurd," to use Dubos' word? Very likely, in the sense of becoming unhealthily distorted. Crete may have been both wealthy and civilized, but it also may have been fragile. A society like the Minoan not only must have stimulated a great increase in population, but ultimately must have required such an increase to support its fine palaces, its priesthood and its nobility. To maintain such a structure takes a lot of people.

It is reasonable to suppose that during the 16th Century B.C. Crete began to suffer, for the first time, some symptoms of social strain. Overcrowding could have been the first sign. And there is evidence of it in increased Minoan expansion into other places. Thera could be an example. Even if the population of Akrotiri was smaller than Marinatos thought, it was still a sizable place. And it may not have been the principal town on Thera. A larger one may be lying somewhere else right now, undiscovered and unsuspected under its load of ash. Thera as a whole may have been home for many thousands at the time of its destruction.

Perhaps the system was flexible enough and efficient enough to tolerate a larger and larger palace load supported by a larger and larger population. It could have done that for a time, perhaps for a long time, but only if the system continued to tick like a watch, all its parts meshed for maximum productivity. This would have required a clear identity of roles in the system (social stratification), strong central and religious authority, ingrained obedience—and probably considerable movement overseas to act as a safety valve by relieving population pressures.

At the same time another unhealthy influence in the system may have manifested itself in the form of a gradually increasing flow of wealth, property and power into the hands of fewer and fewer people. This is the kind of "bad" fallout from an efficient and ap-

Therans slept on beds like this: a hide laced to a wood frame. Reconstruction became possible when excavators at Akrotiri found the ghost of a bed —a space left empty in the volcanic ash after the bed's actual materials had disintegrated. By filling the space with plaster, experts made a model of the original, on which this copy is based.

parently "good" system that leads to the distortions —or absurdities—identified by Dubos. Such concentrations are common in human society. The Greeks, some hundreds of years later, would find themselves dealing with the problem—violently—over and over again. So would the Romans, where huge sections of the country eventually wound up in the hands of a few enormously wealthy landowners.

More people, a heavier load to be supported at the top, less to go around at the bottom. Even that can be tolerated for a time if the redistributive system is working at its most efficient level. But the more complicated the system becomes, the more susceptible it is to an uncomfortable nudge. The dependence of modern society on cheap energy sources is a good example of this, particularly when the jarring threat of an embargo by a foreign oil-producing nation suddenly makes clear how distorted and fragile the system is. Similarly hidden but growing ills in that marvelous Minoan machine could have sent it reeling as the result of a sudden and unexpected nudge. Positive feedback works as well downward, to accelerate disintegration, as it does upward.

If we take a large gulp and concede, as some archeologists maintain, that damage was done to the Minoan palaces and towns by a combination of earthquakes and tsunamis stemming from the blast on Thera; if we assume that most, if not all, of Crete's ships were swamped in the harbors around the island, crippling her defenses and reducing her ability to trade overseas; if we assume that the agricultural basis of the country's economy was jolted by a disastrous ash-fall that blanketed the eastern half of Crete; if, in short, we presume a number of volcanic events on Thera doing one thing or another to start a downward slide in the Minoan economy, then we begin to see how the social structure could have collapsed at a later time as an indirect result of those events. This collapse could have been brought about through internal violence, through conquest from overseas, through a cause we are not yet aware of, perhaps through a combination of these forces.

More and more it begins to look now as if the actual destruction of the palaces and villas on Crete was the work not of volcanoes but of men. What men we do not know, whether desperate and rebellious Minoans or invading Greeks.

What is clear is that after 1450 B.C., despite all the calamities, the population on Crete was not wiped out. Minoans remained on Crete. They continued to till their farms and continued to occupy their villages, but probably in sharply reduced numbers. There were squatters living in some of the palaces off and on, but the palaces—as palaces—were abandoned and were never rebuilt. The sole exception was Knossos. Somehow escaping the general destruction that swept the others away, Knossos seems to have become the center from which control of all Crete was exercised. The controllers were Mycenaean Greeks. They spared Knossos because, logically enough, they wanted to use it themselves.

For two or three hundred years prior to the collapse of the palace system, the Minoan and Mycenaean civilizations had been in increasingly close cultural and commercial contact—headed toward some kind of inevitable confrontation as each expanded. For a long time the Minoans had been the dominant influence in the Aegean. They were the ones with the more elaborate culture, the seafarers, the merchants who knew the world. The Mycenaeans, by contrast, had started as landsmen. But they were restless, aggressive and very enterprising. Gradually they began going to sea too. By 1500 B.C. they were themselves well established as traders. By 1450 B.C. they were in a position to take over Crete—if the Minoans gave them an opportunity to move in. The eruption on Thera may have supplied that chance by fatally weakening Minoan society.

A Mycenaean presence at Knossos after 1450 B.C. is certain: the whole atmosphere and flavor of the place changed, reflecting—in British archeologist Sinclair Hood's words—an "era of chill military grandeur." The Mycenaean Greeks were a conspicuously warlike people. They left a great many weapons behind them. They added to the palace. They introduced a new pottery style. Most significant of all, some of the clay tablets found at Knossos and dating from the time of this late occupation were deciphered not long ago; they turned out to be written in the language of the Mycenaeans—proto-Greek!

The Mycenaeans remained in control at Knossos for nearly a century. Then, about 1380 B.C., the so-called last palace at Knossos was destroyed. Again, who destroyed it is not known. It could have been Mycenaeans fighting with one another; it could have been rebellious Cretans trying to overthrow a regime of domineering outsiders. In either case the day of the palaces was finally over. What Evans found when he first started to probe the ruin at Knossos was the result of that final spasm.

Nothing comparable ever replaced the palace society, although Cretans continued to live on Crete, preserving their customs, their religion and their language down to Classical Greek times. But with the downfall of the last palace at Knossos, nearly 2,000 years of Minoan civilization came to an end.

From Thera
Self-portraits
in Frescoes

Far more varied and complete than anything ever found on Crete itself, the Minoan-style frescoes that Greek archeologist Spyridon Marinatos unearthed on the island of Thera are among the most extraordinary works of ancient art ever discovered. The wall paintings are not only extremely beautiful in themselves, they also reveal and confirm things about daily life in the 16th Century B.C. Aegean that before their discovery could only be surmised: that shepherds wore fur capes, that boys went in for boxing, that women carried jars on their heads, that cheese making was a widespread dairy activity.

In stunning contrast to such everyday vignettes is the naval scene (pages 114 and 115), with its flotilla of ships —the first detailed archeological evidence of what Minoan vessels were like. Nobody could possibly have imagined those fantastic craft, with golden lions on their sterns, and their bows—embellished with images of birds, blossoms and butterflies—tapering almost to needle points. Also unique is the battle scene (page 119), with its drowning sailors and platoons of infantrymen marching off to war.

The verve with which Minoan artists rendered animals comes through with electric force in a fresco of a pair of prancing oryx. Below a border of blue leaves is an irregular background in red—a widely used Minoan motif.

A superb fresco of two graceful
youngsters sparring says that boxing
was a popular Minoan sport. Naked
except for a loincloth, each fighter
wears a glove on his right hand only;
presumably the left was used for
parrying. Spyridon Marinatos, who
discovered the wall painting and
reconstructed missing portions of the
figures, believed the youths were of
noble blood; boys of lesser birth would
not have owned the gold bracelet
and earring, nor the lapis lazuli
necklace worn by the boxer at left.

In one of the best-preserved frescoes
yet found, a Theran youth holds two
strings of mackerel. The fact that the
heads of all three subjects on these
pages are painted in blue created
speculation that they represent young
gods, since divinities in the eastern
Mediterranean often were portrayed
with blue hair or beards. But Marinatos
concluded that the blue represented
short stubble on the boys' heads
—shaved except for a few long locks.

Part of a wall painting nearly 20 feet long, this extraordinary scene is packed with information for scholars to interpret. Some archeologists believe that its setting is Libya on the African coast, a country with which the Minoans are known to have been in contact. This interpretation is strengthened by the antelope fleeing from the lion (upper left) and by the marsh (shown in pink) bordering a river. These features would be found in Libya, not on Crete or Thera. Also significant is the distinctive clipped hair style of the people both on shore and in the ships; Minoans rarely wore their hair this way but Africans did. It is impossible to say what event has been memorialized here. The tranquil atmosphere of the fresco suggests that the ships' passengers, dressed in white robes, are nobles or priests setting out on a diplomatic or religious mission. The vessels themselves, with their extended bows and rich decoration, are extraordinarily revealing. The two at the right clearly show how they were propelled: by oarsmen who sat in a tight row directly beneath the passengers. Totally unexpected is the fact that the oarsmen are faced in the direction the ship is moving, leaning forward and pushing on their oars, rather than rowing in the more usual way, sitting with their backs to the bow and pulling at each stroke. The smaller boat at the lower left, however, is powered in the conventional fashion: by oarsmen facing the stern.

These three ladies all come from Thera.
The one at far left is apparently engaged in
a religious rite. She wears a priestess'
enveloping gown and carries an offering
in a silver vessel. The other two are
fashionable ladies of the period. Narrow-
waisted and clad in long, flounced skirts,
they wear open-fronted boleros. Minoan
artists usually painted their women
full-breasted, but even so the bosom of
the bending woman at right seems extreme.
All three are wearing vivid make-up:
reddened lips and face coloring.

Lilies are a recurrent motif in Theran art. Those in the fresco below cover the walls of this small room. Some are shown in bud, others just opening, still others—with curled-back petals—in full bloom. Swallows gracefully flit about. The strangely colored rocks are thought to represent the multihued volcanic landscape of ancient Thera.

Three themes enliven this fresco. At top are pastoral scenes: from right to left, herdsmen, two peasant girls balancing jars on their heads and tunic-clad Africans—possibly Libyans. Below them, spear-bearing soldiers carrying large body shields march off to war. At bottom a beachfront assault is repelled with at least three casualties.

Chapter Five: The Rise of the Mycenaeans

Who were the Greeks?

Of the many sticky questions encountered in the study of Aegean civilization, this is one of the stickiest. Unlike the Minoans, who say little enough (and that only indirectly through archeology) about their origins, and nothing at all directly (since we cannot read their writing), the Greeks do talk about themselves. In fact, they talk a great deal. The problem is to interpret what they say.

Our knowledge of Greek origins, as told by Greeks, comes from three main sources. The first, and most reliable, dates from the Fifth Century B.C. and comes to us in the clear and educated voices of two historians: Herodotus and Thucydides. The second, from the Eighth Century B.C., finds the poet Homer talking about Greeks. Finally, going back to the 13th and 14th centuries B.C., Greeks speak once again in the household notes and palace accounts that were kept by the great Mycenaean lords. Back of that, Greeks themselves say nothing.

Of the lot, Thucydides is the one who addresses himself most conscientiously to the questions we are interested in: What happened, how and when? He was the first professional historian of the Western world—a modern man, our intellectual contemporary, though he lived about 2,400 years ago. He was sophisticated, curious, his thought processes very much like our own. He based his conclusions about events on logic, on common sense, on personal observation and interviews, and on the best interpretation he could make of the muddled legacy of myth that was handed down to him.

Myth is history—if it can be interpreted properly. Thucydides did his best. He was a literate man living in a literate society. However, for the origins of his people he had to look back 300 years to Homer (who was probably an illiterate and not at all interested in history in the modern sense), then back once again, across a further 400 years of almost total darkness, before he could reach another literate civilization constructed by his own ancestors, the Mycenaeans.

Thucydides never got there. The further back he went, the deeper became the swamp of verbal tales, heroic deeds, movements of peoples, long-tangled genealogies, half-remembered wars and settlements, invasions, flights, marriages—all of it invariably ending up on the doorstep of the gods, to whom every Greek of any pretension traced his ancestry.

A Classical historian trying to work his way patiently backward through time, generation by generation, invariably bumped into Heracles or Aphrodite just when he should have encountered the Mycenaeans. No wonder Thucydides could not see them. Nor, for a long time, could anybody else. Not until after Schliemann had discovered gold at Troy and Mycenae, and a concerted attack had been mounted by scholars and archeologists on the riddle of Homer and the pre-Homeric past, did the reality of Mycenaean civilization begin to emerge. It then developed that the *Iliad*, for all its distortions, could throw light on the vanished Mycenaean world.

At this point it is worth setting down again briefly just what the *Iliad* is. It is an adventure story, a tale handed down by verbal tradition from one bard to an-

Punctuating the defensive walls of Mycenae, erected in 1250 B.C., a monumental sculpture of two lions, each 10 feet high, crowns the entryway to the citadel. The ring of stonework beyond the wall was built to protect a cluster of royal shaft graves excavated by Heinrich Schliemann in 1876. In the far distance sprawls the fertile Argive Plain.

Exquisitely carved, this amethyst gem, only about one third of an inch in diameter, may be the portrait of an early Mycenaean king whose features —long straight nose, high cheekbones— are obviously Greek. Since the artisan worked without a magnifying glass, the fineness of detail is astonishing.

other over a period of several hundred years before reaching its last interpreter of record: Homer. Its subject is a large naval expedition undertaken by a coalition of Mycenaean barons (see box, page 23) in about 1250 B.C. to a place near the Anatolian coast that the Greeks called Ilios (hence the poem's title: the *Iliad*). Ilios is known to the Western world as Troy. The celebrated siege of Troy, the hand-to-hand combats that swept back and forth below its lofty walls, the tricky penetration of those walls by the device of a hollow wooden horse full of Greek soldiers, the destruction of Troy as a result of that deception —all these events have been preserved in Western literature because of the masterful way they were told by Homer. Admittedly Homer garbled them. It would be a surprise if he did not, since they deal with a society that had passed away 400 years before he was born, a society he did not understand and whose very existence was unknown to him.

That is what everyone had missed for so long: that there was a Greek civilization, long before Homer, long before Troy, that the *Iliad* reflected only a distorted memory of it. As that early Greek world now begins to reveal itself, it turns out to have been larger, richer, and far more complicated than anything Homer or his successors imagined.

Properly the civilization should be called Helladic. That is the name given to the entire cultural sequence that struggled slowly out of the Stone Age on the Greek peninsula, flowered there and expired in about 1100 B.C. The name Mycenaean applies only to the last phase of Helladic culture, a period that ran from about 1600 to about 1100 B.C.

The people who lived in Greece during the late neolithic were probably an older population of resident hunter-gatherer-fisher types mixed with newer-style farmers who had moved in from the east and made the old hunting way outmoded. Farming, and the village life that grew up around it, may have been established as early as 7000 B.C. By 3000 B.C., notably in the Peloponnesus, the triple influence of vine, olive and metals had begun to supply the same stimulating ferment that was sparking progress in the nearby Cyclades and on Crete.

Were those mixed Peloponnesians "Greeks"? That depends on what we mean by the term. Usually it is understood to mean Greek-speaking peoples. Although the incoming eastern farmers may well have spoken an Indo-European dialect of some kind, they may not have spoken Greek for the simple reason that nobody in the world then did: Greek had not yet been invented. So, the question becomes: Was the language invented (or, more properly, evolved) right there in Greece, with some outside nudges over a period of about 5,000 years? Or was it introduced, as some think, around 2000 B.C. by intruders, also Indo-European speakers, who began making their way into the lands bordering the Aegean at that time?

This was a period of turbulence and much movement over wide areas. Troy V fell at about this time, apparently captured by outsiders who built a far finer and larger citadel of their own: Troy VI. Other groups apparently moved on into Greece, bringing with them cultural traits suggesting that, like the new arrivals in Troy, they too came from Anatolia or points farther east and north.

Evidence for this infiltration into Greece is not exactly overpowering, but it is there. A few long-established population centers were overrun and destroyed, just as Troy V was. Notable among these was Lerna, one of the largest and oldest towns in the Peloponnesus. Shortly after the fall of Lerna, pottery from Greek graves began to have an Anatolian look.

From such shreds of evidence it is possible to speculate that a people speaking an Anatolian language found their way into Greece just before or just after 2000 B.C. If so, in due course the invaders would have blended in with the locals to different degrees in different ways in different places. After a few centuries the blend—shaken and smoothed—would have emerged as what we now call the Mycenaeans. (Homer called them Achaeans; in many modern works the two terms are interchangeable.)

But did those Mycenaeans speak an early form of Greek? That is the key question, and it was not answered until the 1950s, although arguments about it had been going on since 1900, when Arthur Evans discovered a hoard of clay tablets on Crete, baked hard and preserved by the great fire that consumed the palace at Knossos. These tablets were in an unknown script and an unknown language. The best that Evans could do with them was sort them into two types to which he gave the names Linear A and Linear B. Of the two, Linear A was the older and the scarcer, dating to the 17th Century B.C. Only 300 tablets inscribed with it have been found. By contrast, at Knossos alone more than 3,000 of the Linear B type dating to the 14th Century B.C. were found. Linear A and Linear B were clearly related; they have in common a number of signs. But nobody had the faintest idea what those signs meant or even for what language family they were designed. For decades the tablets sat, inscrutable.

In 1939 the American archeologist Carl Blegen decided to excavate a Mycenaean site in the southwest Peloponnesus. He was looking for a mysterious and elusive place called Pylos, the reputed home of Nestor, one of the Mycenaean heroes who went off to fight at Troy. Nestor figured importantly in the *Iliad*. Homer gave him a large role as the wisest of the heroes, full of sage advice. Like so many old men, Nestor was rather windy, but for all that an important figure because he was the ruler of an important state: "sandy Pylos."

The trouble was that—unlike Mycenae (Agamemnon's home), Ithaca (Odysseus' home), Sparta (Menelaus' home) and other places from the *Iliad*—nobody knew where Pylos was. Even in Thucydides' day nobody knew.

Blegen rediscovered Pylos. Moreover, he found there another hoard of priceless Linear B tablets, about 600 of them (the count later rose to more than 1,000). The discovery was enthralling but bewildering. Did it mean that the Minoans had occupied the Peloponnesus after all, as Evans had thought? No, the palace did not look Minoan. Rather, it seemed to follow a Mycenaean model: a kingly residence built around a large columned central hall called a megaron. But then, what were Linear B tablets—presumably Minoan because hitherto they had been unearthed only on Crete—doing there?

In 1952 a young English architect and amateur cryptographer, Michael Ventris, decided that the combined haul of Linear B tablets from Knossos and Pylos was large enough to warrant an all-out effort at deciphering them. After some false starts he decided to see what would happen if he assumed that the language was a form of Greek. Dramatically, Linear B began to crack. Ventris, along with a co-worker, John Chadwick, announced that Linear B had been partially deciphered and that the language was a primitive version of Classical Greek.

A respectable minority of scholars disagrees with Ventris, who unfortunately was killed in a motor accident shortly after publishing his first paper and was unable either to defend his findings or continue his work. Most experts, however, agree with Ventris and consider his achievement one of the great breakthroughs in understanding Aegean culture. It also answers the question left hanging a few paragraphs back: Did the Mycenaeans speak Greek? The answer is yes. Not only did they speak and write Greek in Pylos, they also spoke and wrote it on Crete (on the evidence of the Linear B tablets found at Knossos), a fact that nails down Mycenaean occupation of Knossos after 1450 B.C. What other explanation could there be for keeping Minoan palace records in Greek?

So, the Mycenaeans spoke Greek or proto-Greek. Furthermore, they emerged as Mycenaeans in a country that had originally spoken something else, as indicated by the persistence of certain place names in Greece. The names of rivers, mountains, local deities, towns, even trees and shrubs, are phenomenally durable. Newly arrived people tend to accept the names they find, rather than attempt to change them. Throughout Greece are words ending in "nthos" or "ssos" (Kórinthos and Parnassós are examples) that are of non-Greek or pre-Greek origin and that may go back thousands of years before Mycenaean times. The Mycenaeans simply swallowed those very ancient words, as did the Classical Greeks 1,500 years later—as do modern Greeks today.

What else those proto-Mycenaeans brought with them besides their language is difficult to say. Helladic culture was already in existence. They simply added themselves to it. A new form of pottery, Minyan ware (page 34), began to show up in Greece shortly after the end of the Third Millennium; the proto-Mycenaeans may have been responsible for that. Otherwise their appearance seems only to have coincided with a general damper that was put on cultural progress at the time. It is tempting to blame them —blame the unsettling effects of their arrival—for that damper. But there is no direct evidence that this was so. Certainly they were a disturbing element, but it is not proper to charge them with an overall slowdown of cultural development at the beginning of the Middle Bronze Age. Mere invasion, it seems, is not all that significant in large cultural trends. There were other confusing elements of the time, not decipherable today, that interfered with the orderly feedback process of development and that, for some reason, were more serious on the mainland than they were on Crete. The result was that the Minoans got a cultural jump on the Mycenaeans that they would hold for several hundred years.

Prior to the cultural slump on the Greek mainland there had been a period of some prosperity and close relationship with the Cycladic islands. Things were looking up, culture was on the march. But the fall of Lerna was symptomatic of the general period of decline that followed. The towns were small and scruffy, the art uninspired. The inhabitants interred their dead in cist graves like those in the Cyclades, and the low quality of their society is reflected in the low quality of their grave goods.

Then something began to stir again. Island contacts were reestablished beginning around 1650 B.C. Energetic local dynasts began making their presence

The Riddles of Aegean Writing

At some point after 2000 B.C. writing reached Crete. Where it came from—whether from Mesopotamia or from Egypt—is not known. But, like other developments on the island, it succeeded in going its own way.

There were at least three distinct systems. In an early form Minoan writing consisted of hieroglyphs—pictures of familiar shapes such as humans, animals, weapons or utensils. They appear on the six-inch clay disk at right, found at Phaistos and dating from about 1700 B.C. The spiral inscription on the disk includes 45 different symbols, some used repeatedly. The inscription seems to be separated into words or phrases, but their meaning is still unintelligible.

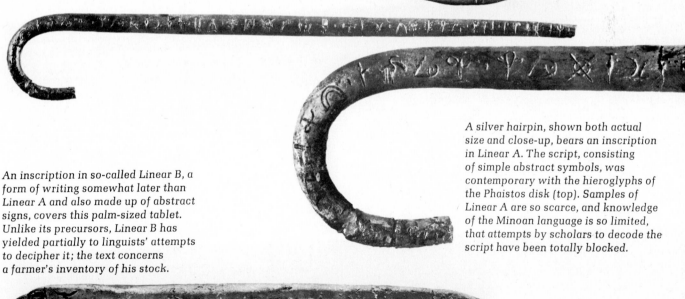

An inscription in so-called Linear B, a form of writing somewhat later than Linear A and also made up of abstract signs, covers this palm-sized tablet. Unlike its precursors, Linear B has yielded partially to linguists' attempts to decipher it; the text concerns a farmer's inventory of his stock.

A silver hairpin, shown both actual size and close-up, bears an inscription in Linear A. The script, consisting of simple abstract symbols, was contemporary with the hieroglyphs of the Phaistos disk (top). Samples of Linear A are so scarce, and knowledge of the Minoan language is so limited, that attempts by scholars to decode the script have been totally blocked.

felt. They were powerful, selfish, determined men—great fighters, ruling in a society that appeared to consist exclusively of nobles and peasants. The nobles got the best of everything; the peasants did what they were told. Evidence of this state of affairs was dramatically revealed when Schliemann stumbled over the shaft graves at Mycenae. Although he believed they were the graves of the people who built the fortress that still stands there, it is now clear that the graves date from 1600 to 1500 B.C. and that the fortress was not built until 250 years later.

The shaft-grave diggers were immensely wealthy. The contents of the five graves that Schliemann found, plus a sixth that was discovered later, make that dazzlingly clear. Not only was the booty very great, it was also very beautiful—and it came from everywhere. There were precious stones from the Near East, silver from Anatolia, glass ornaments and alabaster from Crete, drinking cups made of ostrich eggs from Egypt or Nubia, ivory from Syria, thousands of amber beads from northern Europe and innumerable objects made of gold. There were golden masks, crowns, diadems, vases, drinking cups, rings, arm bands, necklaces, belt knobs, disks, leaves, fish, stars and miniature buildings—all cut from sheets of gold that had been hammered very thin. The people in the graves were almost literally clothed in gold. And their preoccupation with war was clearly indicated by dozens of great bronze swords and magnificently inlaid daggers.

How had all that fabulous wealth been assembled? And—considering how long and assiduously the ignoble profession of grave robbery has been practiced—was not Schliemann's find just a sample of similar great wealth that must have been stored up by other 16th Century Mycenaean lords? To answer the second question, almost certainly yes. Another somewhat less rich, and older, group of graves was discovered in 1951 at Mycenae. Still others have turned up elsewhere in Greece.

These treasures speak eloquently of the movement out into the world of the Mycenaeans (and we can now so call them, for it is generally accepted that the Mycenaean Age began with the period of the shaft graves). American archeologist Emily Vermeule believes that much of the Mycenaeans' early wealth was assembled by force of arms rather than by quiet trading. The swords in the graves back her up; these people were aggressive and determined, more so than the cultured Minoans with whom they were just beginning to come into close contact. Some of the shaft-grave material, in fact, comes from Crete. Some of it is of domestic make, but patterned on Minoan models, suggesting that the Mycenaean princes who collected this treasure may have also collected a few Minoan artisans on their travels.

Those bold 16th Century B.C. barons built the cultural platform on which the later Mycenaean civilization would stand. Mrs. Vermeule identifies five reasons for their success:

First, they were not too many to start with—a close-knit class, many of them probably related. Well armed and overbearing, they found it easy to move in on the local peasantry and set themselves up as overlords wherever they pleased. Greek myth is full of such tales: a prince or king with a band of followers imposing himself on a region and ruling it thereafter. This pattern continued, surprisingly, late into the Mycenaean period, even when Greece had grown much more crowded and the great lords more

Text continued on page 130

Stone Beehives for the Royal Dead of Mycenae

A walled walkway, or dromos, leads to a massive door that is the entrance to the Treasury of Atreus, buried in a hillside at Mycenae.

Late in the 15th Century B.C. the Mycenaeans began to abandon the old custom of putting royal corpses at the bottoms of deep shaft graves, and turned to a new form of interment: the tholos tomb. A beehive-shaped affair made of cut stone, it got its name from the Greek word meaning round or vaulted building. The supreme ex- ample of the tholos is the so-called Treasury of Atreus—named for a man the later Greeks believed had been a king at Mycenae.

Tholoi were usually built nestled in hillsides; when completed, they were mounded over with earth. The larger, more imposing ones had walled walkways leading to their entrances (*above*). Inevitably, the sites of the finest tholoi have been easy pickings for grave robbers. For modern archeology, the losses are immeasurable; if the older shaft graves were rich in treasure (*pages 145-153*), how much more so must have been the tombs built for rulers far wealthier and far more powerful than the earlier kings.

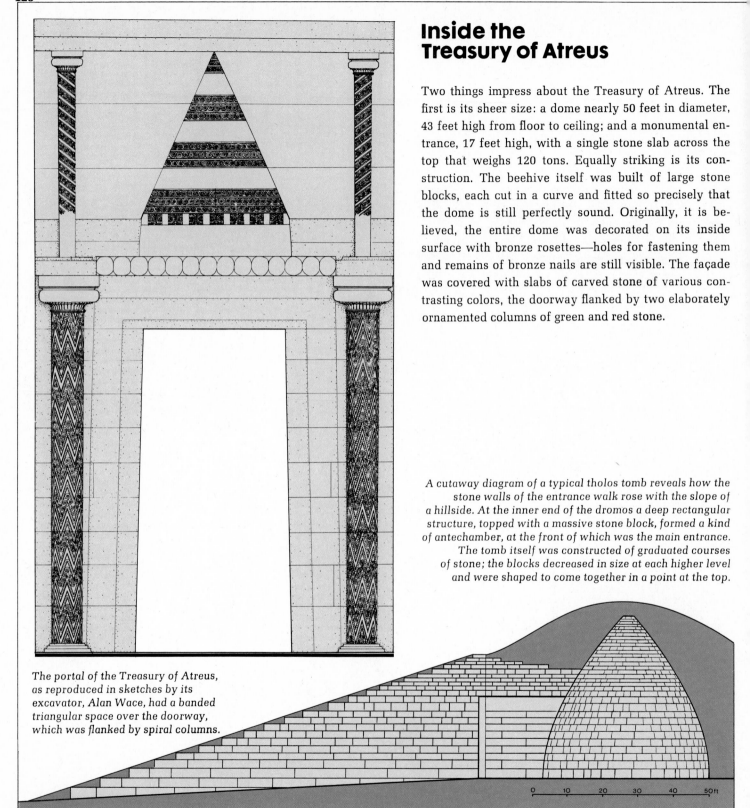

Inside the Treasury of Atreus

Two things impress about the Treasury of Atreus. The first is its sheer size: a dome nearly 50 feet in diameter, 43 feet high from floor to ceiling; and a monumental entrance, 17 feet high, with a single stone slab across the top that weighs 120 tons. Equally striking is its construction. The beehive itself was built of large stone blocks, each cut in a curve and fitted so precisely that the dome is still perfectly sound. Originally, it is believed, the entire dome was decorated on its inside surface with bronze rosettes—holes for fastening them and remains of bronze nails are still visible. The façade was covered with slabs of carved stone of various contrasting colors, the doorway flanked by two elaborately ornamented columns of green and red stone.

A cutaway diagram of a typical tholos tomb reveals how the stone walls of the entrance walk rose with the slope of a hillside. At the inner end of the dromos a deep rectangular structure, topped with a massive stone block, formed a kind of antechamber, at the front of which was the main entrance. The tomb itself was constructed of graduated courses of stone; the blocks decreased in size at each higher level and were shaped to come together in a point at the top.

The portal of the Treasury of Atreus, as reproduced in sketches by its excavator, Alan Wace, had a banded triangular space over the doorway, which was flanked by spiral columns.

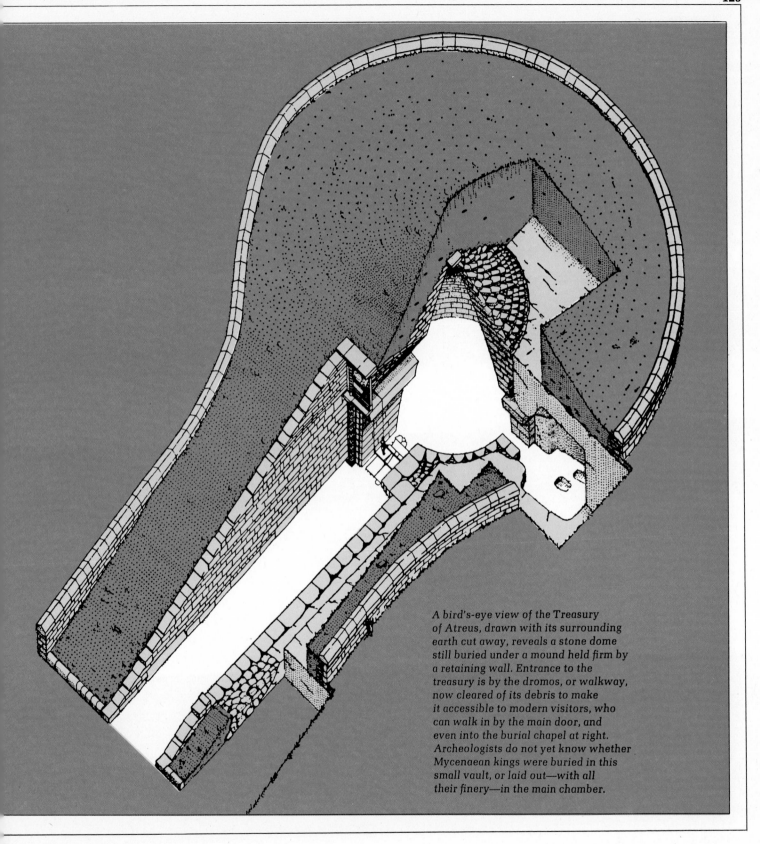

A bird's-eye view of the Treasury
of Atreus, drawn with its surrounding
earth cut away, reveals a stone dome
still buried under a mound held firm by
a retaining wall. Entrance to the
treasury is by the dromos, or walkway,
now cleared of its debris to make
it accessible to modern visitors, who
can walk in by the main door, and
even into the burial chapel at right.
Archeologists do not yet know whether
Mycenaean kings were buried in this
small vault, or laid out—with all
their finery—in the main chamber.

numerous and more jealous of their domains. As late as 1300 B.C. a prince from the north named Neleus found things difficult at home, so he walked into the Peloponnesus and established himself as the lord of an older community that had been there for centuries. Neleus' kingdom would become Pylos, already mentioned for its treasure of Linear B tablets. His son Nestor was ruling there when it came time to gird up and go off to Troy. By then the entire countryside around Pylos had been welded into a strong state ruled from Nestor's palace.

The second reason for the Mycenaeans' success, according to Emily Vermeule, was their sound knowledge of metal technology, along with their skill in exploiting local ores.

Third, they were experienced and innovative fighters, quick to adapt new techniques to their own use. They had the long sword early and were the first in Greece to use the war chariot.

Fourth, they had a strong bent for trade and had the wit to pursue it where the markets were best.

Finally, they were extremely bold in their foreign contacts. They did not hesitate to go anywhere.

Such were the energetic and aggressive people who poured so much of their energy into becoming rich, then poured so much of their riches into deep burial shafts when they died. Those shafts were rectangular, dug straight down into the ground, often into the soft rock, to a depth of 15 to 25 feet. The bottom sections were faced with brick or stone to about shoulder height and a layer of pebbles placed on the floor. The corpse was then lowered, his glittering goods arranged around him, his body often strewn with small gold ornaments. Next a roof of heavy logs was placed on top of the low wall at the bottom of the shaft. Then the shaft, above the logs, was filled with earth, and a headstone placed on the top.

Shafts were used more than once. The six in the Mycenae grave circle contained 19 corpses altogether: eight men, nine women and two children. The site probably was the burial ground of whatever dynasty was in control of Mycenae at the time. For every new death it was necessary to dig out all the earth, repair the log roof if it had fallen in, clean up the burial chamber, deposit the new arrival with his or her effects and fill up the hole again. A big job. Apparently too big a one, for the shaft design fell out of favor and royalty began experimenting with a new kind of burial chamber whose origins are equally unclear.

This was the tholos tomb, a beehive-shaped affair made of dressed stone (page 127). A tholos usually was built in the side of a hill with a passageway and a monumental entrance door leading to it. The lower courses of a tholos were set below ground level in a deep cutting made in the hillside. As the sides rose up in smaller and smaller circles, earth was packed in all around the outside of the growing dome.

This construction was exceptionally solid, but protection against thieves was more theoretical than actual. Many of the tholoi were so large that their tops often stuck out of the ground. It was no great job to find a tholos, stealthily dig around to locate the entrance and then make one's way inside. Tholoi were robbed repeatedly. Even so, the value of their contents apparently was so immense that robbers through the centuries were constantly overlooking things. When the largest and finest of all tholos tombs, the so-called Treasury of Atreus at Mycenae, was carefully sifted and resifted by archeologists, they still found bits of gold and other valuables scattered here and there in the rubble.

The Treasury of Atreus is a stunning piece of architecture. It stands virtually intact today, 43 feet high inside, its stonework finely cut and fitted. Its interior facing, it is believed, was once lined with bronze rosettes. Its doorway was flanked by carved columns of red and green stone. The lintel over it, one solid block, weighs more than 100 tons.

This grandest of all tholoi was built shortly after 1300 B.C. A monument to the peaking of Mycenaean culture, it represents several hundred years of multiplier-effect development on the Greek mainland, and throws into sharp focus the fundamental argument between Alan Wace and Arthur Evans as to whether the Mycenaean culture was independent or an offshoot of the Minoan. It is clear today that Wace was right. The very concept of the citadel was Mycenaean. The strong military flavor of the society was Mycenaean. The design of the megaron, or central palace hall, was Mycenaean. What had confused Evans—and still confused others—was the extent to which the Mycenaeans borrowed from Crete.

Stylistically Crete electrified the Mycenaeans. Its art enchanted them. Its grand palaces sent them off on a 250-year-long binge of palace building and fresco painting of their own. Previously, despite their enormous wealth and their prestigious tombs, the Mycenaeans had been rather mingy architects. But, strolling through the maze of corridors and apartments that they were just settling into at Knossos in about 1450 B.C., staring at the wondrous frescoes all about them, the painted columns and decorated floors, the Greeks must certainly have developed ideas for a more grandiose life style at home.

Probably the best place to study a Mycenaean palace and what went on in it is Pylos. Pylos was sacked and burned about 1200 B.C., so thoroughly that it was never rebuilt or reoccupied. As at Knossos, the wood used in its construction and the large oil stores fed a furious fire that baked and preserved those precious Linear B tablets.

Total destruction has made Pylos a much "purer" site than a place like Mycenae, with a more complicated history. Mycenae survived several assaults before falling permanently. After the fall it continued to be occupied for centuries by squatters who tore down, rearranged, cleaned up. Consequently its artifacts, save for a handful, have long since disintegrated, or been carted away and thrown out to disintegrate elsewhere. This has made far more difficult the kind of intimate archeological reacquaintance that could be made at Pylos, which was never cleaned up. Carloads of rubbish blanketed the site when Carl Blegen arrived, giving him an unparalleled opportunity for sifting and analysis.

Pylos had its megaron, the king's central hall where all state business was conducted. An elaborate room, meant to impress, its walls were covered with frescoes. Structural members were brightly painted or ornamented. Furniture, though not abundant, was splendid; according to inventories kept in Linear B, the palace had chairs intricately inlaid with panels of carved ivory and gold. Even the floor was decorated in a bold red and blue pattern with a giant octopus painted in front of the throne. Since King Nestor claimed descent from Poseidon, god of the sea, the octopus on the floor may have been Nestor's way of reminding visitors of his illustrious lineage. Putting it there—where it might have been scuffed,

Nestor's palace at Pylos, long lost, was rediscovered in 1939. On the evidence of site analysis, an artist-member of the archeological team created careful reconstructions, two of which appear on these pages. This painting offers a view of the entrance court, surrounded by a gallery. The main entrance is at right, the throne room at left.

instead of in a wall fresco—may seem out of character for a value-conscious Mycenaean merchant prince. But Mycenaeans went barefoot a good deal of the time, and probably all the time when inside a palace; painted floors could have lasted pretty well.

In the center of the megaron was its circular hearth, 13 feet across. Around it were four ornamented columns that supported a second-floor balcony. The megaron had one entrance, flanked by vestibules occupied by guards or by major-domos whose business was to screen traffic and regulate the flow of petitioners. Beyond the vestibules was a courtyard surrounded by a wall pierced by doors leading to the royal apartments and other parts of the palace. One door, the main entry to the palace, opened onto the street. At one time this entrance was fortified by a tower overlooking a narrow slotlike entrance that turned sharply left as one went out, then ran parallel to the other side of the palace wall. This arrangement was common in ancient fortifications. Not only did it oblige attackers to storm the gate in ones and twos, by forcing them to make their way up this narrow slot, but it also obliged them to approach the door with their right sides exposed to the defenders —since shields were always carried on the left arm.

Nestor apparently considered such precautions unnecessary; his palace was virtually unfortified. It stood near the center of a large domain, in a network of smaller towns and villages that were intricately tied to Pylos by oath, custom, mutual defensive need, fear and strong economic dependence.

Like its Minoan model, a Mycenaean palace was a combination military and administrative center, manufacturing plant and warehouse. (Pylos itself specialized in pottery, a lot of which went up the west coast of Greece and over to Italy and Sicily. When it was destroyed, it had a stock of 2,853 stemmed drinking cups stacked in one room alone.) It was a hive of activity, capable of making everything it needed, from harnesses to armor, including a quantity of extra things for export. The tablets found at Pylos make clear the wide variety of specialists working in the palace. They catalogue the output of these craftsmen, keep detailed inventories, note how much of this went to one man, how much of that came from another, record allotments to be paid out by the palace

King Nestor's throne room was approximately square, with a round hearth in the center and a second story supported by four columns; both the hearth and the column bases are still in place at the site. Minoan influence is obvious in the lavish decorations on walls and ceiling, but the designs themselves are Mycenaean.

and taxes due in. Careful records were kept of everything, down to a notation about two oxen named Glossy and Blackie. Troops were ordered about, and a close check kept on military supplies.

The subsidiary towns in the domain—secondary collecting points for woven cloth, lumber or farm products—were not only necessary for the economic functioning of the whole enterprise, but they were also dependent on the palace for their own protection and for the supplies of raw metal or clay, or whatever key commodity they needed for their work. Something like bronze would have been doled out to them by the palace; they did not have access to such materials directly. The palace—its port, its fleet, its soldier-traders who went voyaging and dealt with foreigners—had such access and in that way kept its own people tied to it. They could not function without it. The palace could not prosper and be strong without them. It levied troops from them, armed them, trained them, and led them in battle. The Mycenaean palace system was the military-industrial complex of its day.

Up to the time of the volcanic eruption on Thera about 1500 B.C. the Minoans were clearly the dominant influence in the Aegean. But the Mycenaeans were pushing out, becoming trade-oriented and expansionist-minded. Their experience as seamen was growing. They were beginning to learn where the best markets and the best sources of raw material were, and going directly to them. They seem to have done this in harmony with the Minoans, perhaps even with their assistance.

But growing economies and growing populations need larger and larger bases. Since Mycenae and Crete were both expanding, it was inevitable that at some point they would collide. The eruption on Thera may have merely hastened the collision. When it came, the contest was not an even one. There has been speculation about a failure of Minoan will, giving rise to a picture of a people that had become so effete and luxury-loving that they more or less abdicated their control of the Aegean and capitulated to the Mycenaeans without a decent struggle. What seems more likely is that Crete was so ravaged economically and politically by the indirect consequences of the Theran eruption that she was

The martial overtones of Mycenaean society are confirmed in both weaponry and art. On the gold signet ring at left, a lone warrior fights off three attackers. Of the two swords at right, the top one is an older Minoan design; the other, a Mycenaean improvement on it. The Minoan version was long and cumbersome, and the tang—or fitting—that connected handle to blade was weak; in combat the sword was apt to break at that point. The Mycenaean tang was much stronger, with more rivets and stout shoulders that further strengthened it.

no match for the Mycenaeans when they moved in.

How this transfer of control was effected is hopelessly blurred. The mainland seems not to have been hit by tsunamis—at least there is no archeological evidence that it was. Nor was there ash-fall; the wind was blowing away from the mainland when the blast came. Certainly the Mycenaeans were aware of the catastrophe. If they did not experience it directly, they could scarcely have avoided learning about it, since they were actively moving about in the Cyclades and, in fact, in regular contact with Crete.

Doubtless they watched events there very closely. It is interesting that they did not move in immediately after the explosion, which suggests that the inherent stability of the Minoan palace system may have allowed Crete to proceed on its own momentum for some years, giving a false picture of the island's health and its ability to recover. The true postblast effects on that intricate redistributive system may not have revealed themselves for a generation or so, by which time the Minoan palace economies may have become large, shaky shells.

It must be remembered that there was no Mycenaean empire during this Minoan crisis period, only a collection of small independent kingdoms, none of them nearly as large as the outwardly powerful ones on Crete. One of them, or a coalition, finally may have decided that Knossos was ripe for the plucking, and moved in. The situation could have been analogous to the takeover of a large floundering corporation by a smaller, more aggressive one with abler management. The Mycenaeans had no wish to destroy the Minoan palace system. They wanted to manage it themselves, clear away the executive deadwood at the top and put its assets to work as part of a larger

and richer enterprise of their own. The corporate headquarters was at Knossos.

What happened at the other Minoan palaces is still a mystery. They were not occupied by Mycenaeans; their ruins do not contain evidences of Mycenaean-inspired Palace style pottery (which was confined to the Knossos area). The invaders may have decided that an island as large as Crete could be managed safely by them only if potential sources of trouble were rooted out. This view could have led to a systematic program of stripping the other palaces of all their wealth and then setting the torch to them. But this explanation does not really satisfy. If Knossos was useful to the invaders, why would not Phaistos or Kato Zakro have been just as useful? If the Mycenaeans were having any success at all in reorganizing and exploiting one part of Minoan society —with its great wealth of manufacturing and artistic expertise, its long commercial experience in many overseas markets—why not all of it? Finally, if there were large and luxurious villas scattered over the island, waiting to be occupied by ambitious invading princelings, why were those destroyed?

If no convincing argument can be found for a rampage by Mycenaean Greeks all over Crete, the only alternative is revolt—a rampage by the Minoans themselves. But whether they were rampaging against foreign or native overseers cannot be established.

Equally perplexing is the final destruction of the palace at Knossos about 1380 B.C. Again there is no way of telling whether this was the work of rebellious Minoans or of invaders fighting invaders. By this time the kingdoms on the mainland had grown considerably in size and were beginning to rub irritatingly against one another. In the process smaller

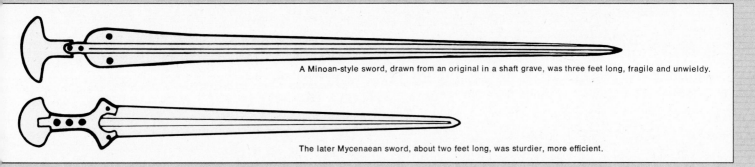

A Minoan-style sword, drawn from an original in a shaft grave, was three feet long, fragile and unwieldy.

The later Mycenaean sword, about two feet long, was sturdier, more efficient.

ones were shaken out or became subservient to a few principal survivors: notably Mycenae, Tiryns, Athens, Thebes and Pylos. Each was a palace-state. The fall of Knossos may reflect an overseas extension of some stateside conflict among some of the larger outreaching Mycenaean kingdoms, perhaps over spheres of trading influence.

Whatever the case, the destruction of Knossos does not mean a Greek departure from Crete; Mycenaeans of some stripe or other stayed on. Homer lists Idomeneus, King of Crete, as one of the commanders who showed up to fight at Troy. Idomeneus was one of the bigger guns in the Greek contingent; he commanded 80 ships and was described as the ruler of "Crete of the hundred cities." He was a Mycenaean.

During the 14th Century B.C. Minoan influence in the Aegean faded to a whisper. That sea became a Mycenaean lake as the mainland palace-states continued to push their ships into all its corners and beyond. They dominated the Cyclades. They established colonies in Rhodes, Miletus and Cyprus. They went to Troy, to Egypt. They set up trading posts in Asia Minor and down in Lebanon at the old Canaanite port of Ugarit. Wealth poured in and the population mushroomed. By 1300 B.C.—on the evidence of great crowding in grave sites—there may have been as many people in Greece as there would be in the great days of Athens 900 years later.

Of all the mainland palace-states, Mycenae grew the fastest. It became a center for working ivory from Syria and for the export of some of the best bronze weapons and pottery of the day. Its citadel stood on a hill overlooking the fertile plain of Argos. Wide expanses of arable land are rare in hilly Greece. In the

Bronze Age they were priceless assets. They provided the space, the men, the farm produce, the network of subsidiary settlements and small productive communities that made the emergence of palace kingdoms possible. From the time it first gained control of the Argive Plain, Mycenae was an important place. By 1300 B.C. it was the most important in Greece.

It is worth a modern visitor's time to linger on at Mycenae in the late afternoon until the other sightseers are gone and he has the site to himself. He can climb up one side of the old fortress and sit on what is left of the great fortification wall, watch the sun go down and listen to the larks singing. And he can have some long Ozymandias-like thoughts about the vanity of men. Below him, inside the walls, is the grave circle from which the gold from the shaft graves was taken, placed there 3,500 years ago by a lost line of grasping kings. Just beyond the walls is another older grave circle excavated in 1952 by two distinguished Greek archeologists, George Mylonas and the late John Papadimitriou. There are 14 shafts here, 24 royal corpses. An older different dynasty, or ancestors of the others? Not far away, buried in a hillside, is the Treasury of Atreus. Descendants or usurpers? Here in this sequence of burials are more than 200 years of aspirations played out by the greatest men in Greece, not a single one of them known by name.

The citadel itself postdates those faceless dynasts. Its most imposing elements were massive walls built of immense irregular blocks of stone, so large and heavy that later Greeks thought they must have been the work of a race of giants. Hence their name, Cyclopean, after the giants described by Homer in the *Odyssey*. Although Mycenae had had fortifications of a sort for centuries, these last and largest and most durable were not erected until about 1250 B.C. This is odd because Mycenae was probably at its most powerful then and should have felt less rather than greater need for such ambitious walls. However, there seems to have been a growing sense of unease among the Mycenaean rulers at about that time, for similar massive fortifications were put up in other places. An obsessive preoccupation with defense is most evident at nearby Tiryns, where in some instances the walls are more than 50 feet thick, with narrow defensive corridors built into them, awkward corners to be turned by invaders.

All this was justified, as it turns out. Beginning shortly before 1200 B.C., in a series of holocausts reminiscent of the disasters that crushed Minoan palace society 250 years earlier, the great Mycenaean palaces were destroyed. For a long time the damage was thought to have been the work of "rude" Dorians flooding into Greece from the north. All the history books of a generation ago made this claim—a few still do—but it no longer stands up.

The Dorians were rude all right, far less civilized than the Mycenaeans, but they did not come in a horde. Nor, probably, did they come from very far away. They trickled in, either pushed along by pressures that are concealed from us today, or simply expanding opportunistically. They were, in fact, Greeks themselves—probably coming from what is now Epirus in northern Greece—the last Greeks to enter the Mycenaean world of southern Greece. They settled where they could, and eventually overran most of the Peloponnesus and the entire western half of Crete. They did not destroy Mycenaean civilization. That was already in the first stages of a complex process of self-destruction when they arrived. They

simply picked up the pieces and emerged as a dominant force some hundreds of years later in Classical Greece. The Spartans, for example, were Dorians.

To find a reasonable explanation for the Mycenaean collapse it is necessary to look deeper and wider, to step back and examine the entire palace system, not only in respect to the mutual relationships of units within it (the various palaces) but in their relationships with the outer world. That way we may recognize a system with a familiar complaint: one whose very success inevitably led to excess, to the kind of "absurdities" that René Dubos identifies.

The Mycenaeans were inherently warlike. They never got on too well with one another, but thrived in an atmosphere of armed, tense watchfulness that periodically broke out in fighting. Greek myth is drenched with accounts of this sort of behavior. At one stage in the evolution of the Mycenaean states this aggressiveness may well have been a positive-feedback factor in their development. Their history between 1600 and 1250 B.C. is one of steadily expanding strength and prosperity. Furthermore, despite their aggressiveness, they did have some capacity to cooperate. An excellent road system testifies to this. So does the fact (if Homer can be elevated to the status of fact) of the expedition to Troy. It consisted of a coalition of armed contingents from no less than 175 different places, led—and properly so—by the head of the largest and most powerful state, King Agamemnon of Mycenae. Somehow a group of mutually mistrustful Greeks managed to pool their energies for the duration of a great piratical expedition, though there were some near-fatal disagreements among them before they were through.

What emerges is a picture of a society that man-

The defensive walls of the citadel at Mycenae were built of Cyclopean blocks of stone, so gigantic that the Classical Greeks believed they could only have been installed by a race of extinct giants. This section of the wall has a paved corridor at its center leading to a secret underground cistern outside the citadel. With the water supply thus available, the fortress was virtually impregnable. Before the cistern was added Mycenae, on a rocky outcrop, was vulnerable to siege.

aged to get on with itself well enough to prosper and expand as long as there was a frontier to absorb the pressures generated by the need for further expansion. That frontier was the large trading world of the eastern Mediterranean into which the Mycenaeans flooded after the fall of the Minoan palace system. It was also a dumping place for excess population, which—following the example of Crete—had also come on the heels of great social success and was now becoming a problem.

Emily Vermeule points out that the late Mycenaeans had an incomprehensibly large surplus balance of payments; archeology shows that they were exporting an immense amount of pottery and other valuables but getting very little durable stuff back. This suggests to her that much of what they were trading for was a perishable commodity such as grain. Presumably mainland Greece, during its late, great Bronze Age days, needed to import food. Arable areas there, like the Argive Plain, though fertile, are not large. Furthermore, they were not intensively cultivated in grain crops since Greece had neither plow nor ox yoke at that time. It stands to reason that the large demands of a palace and a heavy force of non-food-producing craftsmen would have required grain imports—or would have led to a dangerously high level of fighting if those imports were cut off.

What was happening in the outer world that might have affected Mycenaean trade and food imports? As it turns out, plenty. Previously the eastern Mediterranean had been relatively quiet. The Minoans had kept down piracy in the Aegean. Asia Minor was in the iron grip of the Hittite Empire, a large and powerful state with a capital on the lofty plateau of Anatolia. Hittite influence was spreading south into what is now Syria, and beyond to the Canaanite ports on the Lebanese coast. This land had long been under Egyptian control, and in 1288 B.C. a revitalized Egypt under Pharaoh Ramses II went north with a great army in an attempt to crush the Hittites forever. The latter responded on a comparable scale, pouring out of the hills with a mass of ground troops and 3,500 war chariots. The two armies met in an epic but inconclusive struggle in the gorges at Kadesh. The effort so exhausted Ramses that he retired to Egypt, and Egyptian control of the Levantine trading ports faded. Short-term, this was an excellent opportunity for the alert Mycenaeans. They set up trading posts in the Levant, particularly at the Canaanite port of Ugarit, where much evidence of Mycenaean export pottery has been found.

Although the two great powers signed a non-aggression pact after the battle of Kadesh, their rivalry was not really ended. It had, in fact, set in motion forces that would mushroom and prove devastating to orderly trade in the Aegean.

Since neither the Hittites nor the Egyptians were seagoing empires, they recruited navies from those who were. This course gave rise to the so-called Sea Peoples, who were active in the eastern Mediterranean and the Aegean in the last half of the 13th Century B.C. Although their origin is murky in the extreme, they seem to have been confederations of coastal and island peoples, taking advantage of the big struggles on land, lining up on whichever side seemed more lucrative at the moment, engaged in what can best be called organized piracy.

The Mycenaeans, freebooters by instinct, must certainly have become involved in some of those enterprises. The returns were probably good at times, since courageous and opportunistic people have always been able to prosper at the expense of others in periods of maximum confusion. But long-term the effects must have been catastrophic. Ugarit, most cosmopolitan of the Levantine ports, was sacked and burned at the end of the 13th Century B.C., presumably the victim of a mass attack by the Sea Peoples. It never recovered, and an important Mycenaean trade outlet disappeared. The Ionian coast—where there were several Mycenaean colonies, including two important ones at Miletus and Ephesus—was in a turmoil. There were small kingdoms all along this shore, their faces exposed to the threat of piracy, their backs uncomfortably bared to the threat of Hittite interference from the hills behind them.

Hittite might was nothing to trifle with. When the Hittite king spoke, he did so in words of a chilling absolutism; his anger could result in ruthless mass-slaughter and the deportation of entire populations. All this has only gradually come into fascinating focus with the decipherment of Hittite writing. An enormous hoard of Hittite clay tablets has been recovered in recent years, and as scholars slowly plow their way through them a better and better picture emerges of this little-known but potent empire.

But there was one group of people operating down on the Aegean-Anatolian coast to whom the Hittite king spoke in a curiously conciliatory tone. These were the Ahhiyawa, who were making great nuisances of themselves; and the way he dealt with them was entirely at odds with the way he dealt with everybody else. Why did he not break down their gates, murder or flay their men, carry off all their women and property, then burn their communities?

That growing puzzle came to the attention of the

British Homeric scholar Denys Page during many years of puzzling over another problem: Just what was the siege of Troy all about? Did it really happen? If so, were the Mycenaean Greeks involved?

More on those questions in a moment. First hear Page on the subject of the Ahhiyawa. He starts by agreeing with some language experts and Hittitologists that "Ahhiyawa" was the Hittite way of saying "Achaea." On this point he has his adversaries. The American scholar James Muhly, for one, will not make that connection. He insists that the Ahhiyawa were not Achaeans at all, but just another lot of Anatolians struggling along just where they should be: in western Anatolia.

Nevertheless Page has some redoubtable support. And if we grant him his premise (that "Ahhiyawa" equals "Achaea"), then he may be followed along a persuasive argument. In an elaborate analysis of clues from Hittite tablets, he concludes that those Ahhiyawa/Achaeans/Mycenaeans were operating from what is known to have been a Mycenaean base on the island of Rhodes, and the reason the Hittite king dealt with them so gingerly was that he could not get at them. He had to swallow his terrible pride and deal with them as equals, making alliances with them some of the time, complaining reproachfully about their treachery the rest of the time.

So long as the Hittite throne was strong, the Achaeans probably had the best of both worlds, picking the ruler's coastal pocket behind his back, trading with him to his face, hiring out to him as a naval auxiliary during his great efforts against the Egyptians. But this state of affairs did not last long. The Hittite Empire began to unravel with alarming speed about 1200 B.C. In the years just prior to that the Hittites had been having increasing difficulty dealing with the states whose boundaries ran down to the coast. Finally they gave up any effort at controlling them.

Piracy became a way of life in Ionia and the eastern Mediterranean. The Achaeans found themselves in a swirl of other brigands as tough as they were. Although they doubtless were able to survive in that world, the effects back on the Greek mainland were extremely serious. By that time there were large populations in all the palace-states, and a humming mercantilism dependent on placid foreign markets to soak up Mycenaean products in exchange for large supplies of food. Only if that two-way trade could hold up could the Mycenaean palaces continue.

With the eastern Aegean in turmoil it could not. That fact began to be evident as early as 1250 B.C. (and, as in all societies, surely before the protagonists could begin to understand what was about to happen to them). The first symptom, already noted, was the extraordinary precautions some of the Mycenaean cities began taking to make themselves secure by beefing up their fortifications.

This would have been the onset of a period of great tension. Excess populations must have continued to be drained off by movement to overseas Mycenaean towns and trading posts just when freebootery and rapine were changing the complexion of life there. At home there must have been disturbing pileups of export goods, food shortages, unemployment and great civil discontent. Ambitious dynasts are certain to have taken advantage of the situation and begun chopping away at the control of established kings.

This state of affairs begins to show up with increasing clarity in Greek myth—in stories like The Seven Against Thebes (in which a small group of heroes tried to drive a corrupt ruling dynasty from a powerful walled city). That legend is now given historical weight by the knowledge that Thebes was sacked some time between 1250 and 1200 B.C. After Thebes the other palace-states fell like dominoes:

Pylos: sacked and burned just before 1200 B.C., apparently victim of an overwhelming piratical raid.

Gla: a fortified town on an outcrop of land rising from a drained lake bed just north of Thebes; demolished by unknown hands.

Iolkos: farther north in Thessaly; sacked and burned some time between 1200 and 1150 B.C.

Tiryns: near Mycenae in the Peloponnesus; sacked and burned, probably after 1200 B.C.

Mycenae: attacked before 1200 B.C. and all the houses outside the citadel walls destroyed; attacked again just after 1200 B.C. with evidence of further destruction; the citadel itself breached and the palace sacked some 70 years later.

Those were the big ones. Smaller places all over Greece, poorly garrisoned, feebly walled—if walled at all—went up like kindling and vanished.

The dates of these events, all clustering around 1200 B.C., can be approximated fairly closely through a very recent and important development in Greek archeology. During the past couple of decades men like the British scholar Richard Hope Simpson have been tramping about the Greek countryside conscientiously collecting fragments of pottery wherever they found them, and in the process building up a remarkably complete picture of the geography of the Mycenaean world. Big sites are easily identifiable in this way, but so are a great many small ones lost to history. Many are in the Peloponnesus; others are in Attica and in Boeotia, a district north of Attica.

What is interesting about this recent archeological mapping is that it corresponds with surprising accuracy to the so-called Catalogue of Ships from the second book of Homer's *Iliad.* The catalogue carefully lists the names of all the Greeks who participated in the expedition to Troy, and the number of ships contributed by each contingent.

Like the rest of the *Iliad,* the Catalogue of Ships came down to Homer by word of mouth after centuries of repetition, polished and changed by generations of court bards. Two things are remarkable about the list. The first is its strong Boeotian flavor. Whoever first compiled it must have been a Boeotian, for the names of Boeotian towns (most of them small and unimportant) appear more often by far than those from any other district in Greece. This is all the more remarkable when one realizes that in the later days of Classical Greece, Boeotia had become a rural area with somewhat of a country-bumpkin flavor; there would have been no reason for anybody other than a Boeotian to pay so much attention to it.

The second curious thing about the Catalogue of Ships is that its Boeotian emphasis lasted so long, particularly since the Boeotians themselves played no part in the story during the trip to Troy, and almost none after the expedition got there. The reason for the durability of the Boeotian flavor is believed to be that the Catalogue of Ships *was* a catalogue, a mere list of those who went. It did not inspire the poets, who simply memorized it and ran through it by rote when they were performing, then went on to devote their creative skills to more interesting, action-filled parts of the narrative. In that way the catalogue was preserved like a poetical fly in a hunk of more changeable amber that was increasingly rubbed out of shape

An ivory relief of a 1300 B.C. Mycenaean warrior includes a boars'-tusk helmet (page 151), a long spear and a large figure-8 shield. Discovery of such shields in Minoan and Mycenaean art lent credence to Homer's descriptions: the Iliad referred to shields of this type although they had become obsolete and disappeared several centuries before the poet described them.

as time passed, as new lords rose and as new bards warped their songs to massage those new egos.

The timing clue hidden in the Catalogue of Ships is simply that it preserved the names of places that existed at the time the expedition to Troy began. *Before* Troy they existed. *After* Troy many of them did not. For example, Agamemnon went from Mycenae and Nestor went from Pylos. Both came home. Their palaces were struck about 1200 B.C. Therefore, if the *Iliad* is to be taken seriously, the Trojan War took place before 1200 B.C., probably in the neighborhood of 1220 B.C., since that is about the time of the first damage to Mycenae. That would not have happened before the King's departure; if things at home had been that turbulent, he would not have left.

But is the *Iliad* to be believed? This is another absorbing question that has engaged some of the best Classical minds since the time of Thucydides. Interestingly enough, science, which normally would be expected to demolish so fanciful a tale in its entirety, seems to be finding more and more substance to it. Throw out the superhuman, crack open the thick shell of myth and use whatever picks are provided by geography, archeology, and language study to prize out the kernel of truth at the center. The truth is that the *Iliad* does have its roots in the Mycenaean world and was not invented at some later time.

Here Denys Page again speaks eloquently, noting first the large number of place names in the *Iliad*'s Catalogue of Ships. Three fourths of those places, thanks to the work of Hope Simpson and others, are identifiable today. They all reveal themselves, under competent archeological examination, to have been Mycenaean towns.

Reversing that statement puts it even more strongly: no identifiable place in the catalogue is *not* a Mycenaean town. In addition, many have identifying descriptive adjectives attached to them, a bardic characteristic: "sandy Pylos," "rugged Aegilips," "white Oloöson," "windy Enispe." When Enispe is visited—and it does turn out to be windy—it is hard to believe that the descriptions of those places were not handed down by people who knew them and took care to describe them accurately. How long would a poet last, singing to a knowledgeable audience, if he simply faked epithets and, as Page puts it, placed "flowers on a rocky peak and vineyards in a marsh"? Not long. He would have been hooted out of the megaron and probably out of the bard's guild.

To nail down this point, Page then calls attention to the places in the Catalogue of Ships that are not known today. They too have their descriptive epithets, but despite that helpfulness they have stubbornly resisted identification since Thucydides' day. Page goes on: "Nobody supposes that a Boeotian or an Ionian from Asia Minor traveled in the Dark Ages round the mainland, blazing a trail for Baedeker; indeed it is doubtful whether the most tactful tourist would have got far in the Dorian Peloponnesus at that time." The dark age Page refers to is the 400-year period between the Mycenaean collapse and the birth of Homer, when conditions throughout Greece were so chaotic that any stranger would have been murdered before he traveled very far. And yet those unidentifiable places are not only listed but characterized. Clearly they were obliterated during the dark age but remembered by poets from an earlier time.

In short, the *Iliad* shows, both by what is recognizable in it today and by what is no longer recognizable, a consistency that supports the conclu-

sion that its original authors were describing places as they existed in late Mycenaean times.

That finding is made even more likely when one considers the importance of the places Homer describes. When he took over the tale of Troy and shaped it to his own taste, Sparta, Athens, Argos and Corinth were the important states in Greece. Mycenae was a backward little place, Pylos had disappeared completely. How, then, could Homer glorify Mycenae and Pylos, and pay so little attention to contemporary places unless he was singing of a tradition that was more accurate than his own view could possibly be? He himself did not understand this; he was simply inheriting sagas from the past, embroidering them and passing them on, unwittingly dropping telltale clues about their true origin as he went.

There are many such clues. For example, the *Iliad* contains numerous references to the large shields used by the Greek warriors at Troy. They were of a peculiar figure-8 shape, and are described as tower shields, so tall that they were hung from the shoulder by a strap and reached almost to the feet. Such shields did not exist in Homer's day, having long been made obsolete by smaller round ones. His descriptions of those peculiar archaic shields were utterly baffling until excavations at Knossos and in Greece produced pictures of them on pottery and in frescoes. Now it is plain that Homer inherited the details of those shields, and uncomprehendingly but dutifully passed them along.

His references to chariots are equally revealing. By his time chariot warfare was unknown to the Greeks; it had passed into oblivion with the evolution of cavalry and better-equipped foot troops. But the men at Troy had chariots. Unsure of how to explain their employment, Homer often turned them into taxis —vehicles that transported the heroes to the scene of battle, whereupon they dismounted to fight.

Is the Bronze Age in the Aegean reflected in Homer? Indeed yes, in many such revealing slips. He even provides glimpses of conditions at the time of its breakup. Things were beginning to unravel. Thebes had fallen. Trade was in a chaotic state and piracy in the Aegean booming. The Greeks, particularly those in the eastern Aegean, were probably in it up to their necks. Egyptian records note their participation in the two largest piratical adventures ever recorded. One took place about 1190 B.C. when, in a combined operation, an enormous flotilla of Sea Peoples swept south to swamp Egypt. About seven years later another coalition of pirates took on the fading Hittites off the coast of Cyprus. Both forays failed, but for the Hittites and Egyptians those were their last victories. Totally drained, they were unable to hold their empires together; and the long-orderly, long-prosperous trading world of the Bronze Age Aegean fell in ruins.

The story of the siege of Troy can be viewed as a symptom of that spreading ruin, as just another of the organized piratical expeditions of the time—an all-Greek one. Greeks were already operating up and down the Ionian coast, taunting the crumbling Hittites, allying themselves with coastal upstarts, looking for footholds on the coast for themselves. What better way of getting rich than to take a crack at Troy farther up the coast? Troy had been a formidable and rich fortress for centuries. But with her allies in a shambles because of the overall Hittite mess, Troy just might be taken.

There were undoubtedly other Troys, unremembered today because no Homer spoke of them. But Homer chose to speak of Troy, and we can thank him for it. His heroes straggled home, and their arrival focuses another light on the tumult that was beginning to roar over Greece.

Nestor, it is true, came home quietly to Pylos. Apparently his throne had been held secure for him.

Agamemnon, however, got quite a different reception. Although he ruled the greatest state in the Mycenaean world, although he had just won a great war and was laden down with booty, although he was at the head of a war-hardened and victorious army—none of this counted. He strode into his palace and was murdered by a usurper before he even finished taking a bath.

Odysseus had his troubles too. Rivals had swarmed like locusts into his palace on Ithaca. They were eating him out of house and home. It was all his wife Penelope could do to preserve her virtue amid that swaggering throng, who if given the run of the palace much longer would surely have begun fighting among themselves, the victor taking Penelope by force and assuming the throne. It was to this scene that Odysseus came home. Crafty as always, he sneaked in, sized up the situation, then slaughtered all the potential usurpers when he got the chance.

These homecomings, very possibly based on actual events, speak vividly of the turmoil and decay that was beginning to eat away at the Mycenaean palace system as it careened from one coup to another, from one sacking to another—all rising from the system's inability to survive as an organized network of central bureaucracies based on trade. When their world got too unruly, when their trading markets collapsed, so did they.

They went down very fast, in a niagara of positive feedback, each element in the palace system becoming unstuck as the supporting elements gave way. By about 1100 B.C. Mycenaean culture had disappeared. It was replaced by a feudal society of great poverty and much violence. The population plummeted. The survivors holed up in crags, secure both from the dangerous sea and from their equally dangerous neighbors. Artists, having no royal patrons to serve, lost their skills, grew old and died, and nobody replaced them. Similarly with the great masters of pottery and metalwork. The silver and gold needed for an inlaid bronze sword were unobtainable, as often was bronze itself. Palace accounts were not kept; there were no palaces left, no inventories to be recorded nor anybody to read them. Ultimately the ability to read and write was lost along with everything else.

Into this world of splintered, illiterate feudal states the Dorians trickled, adding little to it since they were illiterate themselves. This was the dark age of Greece, darker than the one that descended on Europe after the breakup of the Roman Empire. It lasted for three or four hundred years.

The ever-sober Thucydides, if he could not see the glory of the previous civilization, did see very clearly the dim condition that followed it. He saw the Greeks forced "to carry arms because the places where they dwelt were unprotected, and intercourse with one another was unsafe." He explains that after the Trojan War, Greece "was still subject to migrations and in process of settlement, and hence did not get rest and wax stronger. For not only did the return of the Greeks from Ilios, occurring as it did after a long absence, cause many changes, but factions also began to spring up very generally in the cities; and, in consequence of these, men were driven into exile and founded new cities."

Homer stands with a foot in each of two worlds. One foot is in the dark age. The *Iliad*—with its heightened emphasis on clan structure, valor, pride of place, its ferocious interest in war, its glorification of the warrior and its brutal contempt for the low born, its dismissal of women as chattels—describes a feudal society glued by Homer onto legends and events that took place in a different and earlier society.

With his other foot Homer stands on the threshold of a new Greece, a Greece just emerging with the rebirth of writing and the rise of the city-states. He himself probably could not read or write, but within the next hundred years or so his poems would be set down by others who could. In that way they got into Western literature and have been preserved with little change ever since. Blurred and distorted as they are, they are still the only nonarcheological link between the Greeks of the Classical world and those of the Bronze Age.

It is hard to think of the latter disappearing so violently and so irrevocably. The Greek archeologist George Mylonas, who has devoted a lifetime to the study of Mycenaean civilization, puts it best: "The elation a scholar feels when he traces the beginnings and the development of a culture to its climax gives way to a mood of sadness when, following its decline step by step, he finally points to the inexorable end. But the scholar of Mycenaean culture is cheered by the knowledge that from the ashes of the Heroic Age there flowered another civilization deeply rooted in the Mycenaean achievement and that this, the Age of Perikles and Sokrates, was to provide the foundation for our western civilization."

Masterpieces Recovered from Royal Graves

It took Heinrich Schliemann's discovery of fabulous treasure in the shaft graves at Mycenae to alert the world that there had indeed been a Mycenaean culture, and that—beginning around 1600 B.C.—Mycenae's kings and princes had been storing up wealth at an astounding rate.

What surprises is not so much the amount of gold and crystal and ivory that was collected, but the exceptional quality of the craftsmanship. Here was a society, until then unknown to history, illiterate and presumably backward in other ways, whose members had not only the discernment to appreciate exquisite design and workmanship, but the skill to produce it.

Unlike the finery with which many peoples of the day surrounded themselves, the art of the Mycenaeans was truly their own—not stolen in piratical raids. Some of the objects shown here and on the following pages may well have been made by craftsmen imported from Crete; certainly there are Minoan as well as Egyptian and Levantine motifs in some of the work. But the blend is uniquely Mycenaean.

Carved in ivory, this warrior's head, two inches high, has a protective helmet decorated with curved rows representing boars' tusks. That Mycenaeans did wear such headgear has been confirmed by many tusks found in graves and by Homer's accurate description of the helmets.

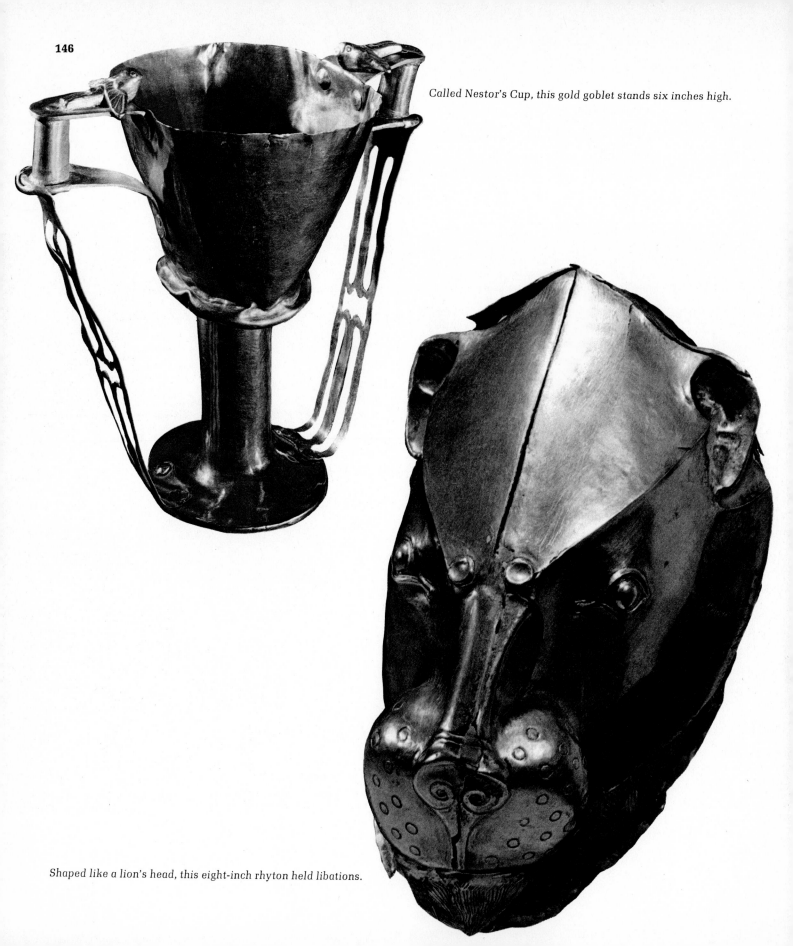

146

Called Nestor's Cup, this gold goblet stands six inches high.

Shaped like a lion's head, this eight-inch rhyton held libations.

Vessels of Gold and Crystal

Royalty at Mycenae was accustomed to the best, especially in its eating and drinking utensils—though the treasures shown here were surely too elegant for everyday use. The lion's-head rhyton *(opposite, bottom)* was a ritual vessel. Nestor's Cup *(opposite, top)*—named by Heinrich Schliemann, who thought it resembled a cup described in the *Iliad*—was made long before Nestor's time; it probably was used only on state occasions. The bowl below was hollowed out by an ingenious method; using common reeds as bits, craftsmen drilled innumerable small cores in the crystal blocks, knocked them out, then rubbed the inside smooth.

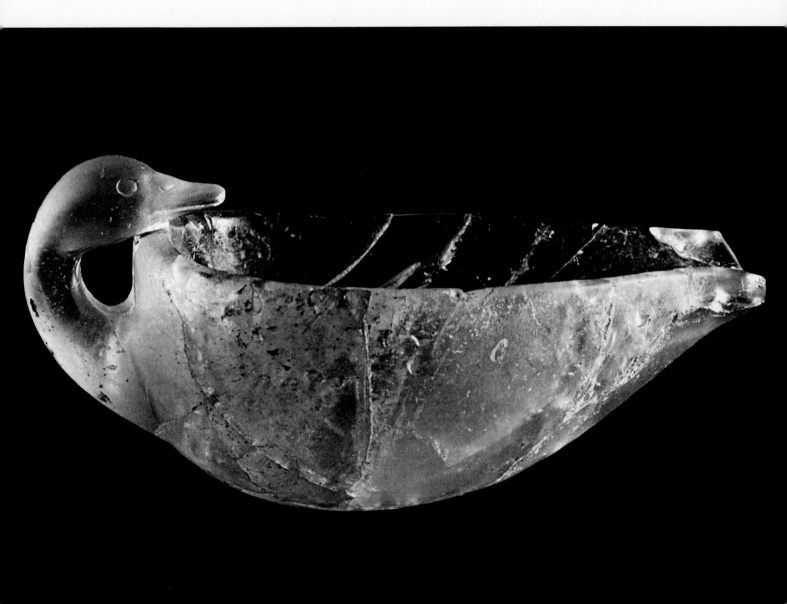

Cut from a single piece of rock crystal, this six-inch-long duck-shaped bowl has sides that taper in thickness to only an eighth of an inch.

Crowns and Jewels of Hammered Gold

Mycenaean graves were rich in gold ornaments, some of *repoussé* open-work like the fancy pinhead opposite top; others, like the flower below it, were made from sheets of gold hammered thin. Gold disks were extremely numerous and presumably were made to be sewn on women's clothing. Of particular interest is the eight-piece diadem below; it is 26 inches wide, far too large for any mortal queen to have worn. Some scholars speculate that such oversized tiaras were designed only to be put in graves: they were laid out on royal female corpses and served much the same symbolic purpose that gold masks *(pages 152-153)* did for kings.

To produce the design on this tiara, a model was first carved in stone or wood, then thin sheets of gold were gently hammered against it.

Palms crown the image of a goddess on this three-inch pinhead.

A lily just three inches long came from a tomb at Volos near Mycenae.

This ornamented disk was among 700 in a single grave.

Inlaid Swords and Bronze Armor

That the Mycenaeans were great fighters is proved by the huge numbers of weapons buried with them. One grave excavated at Mycenae yielded three royal skeletons—interred with more than 90 swords. Some of the weapons were so elaborately made that they were obviously intended not for use in combat but rather for display or ceremonial purposes. The care taken to decorate their blades is extraordinary. A technique called niello was used, in which patterns were gouged into one metal and inlays of contrasting metals hammered into the depressions. Then fantastic designs were delicately incised in the multicolored metal surface.

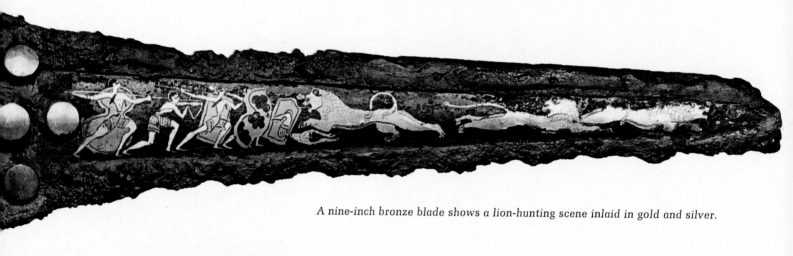

A nine-inch bronze blade shows a lion-hunting scene inlaid in gold and silver.

On a five-inch gold sword handle, a pair of dragons' heads grip the blade.

A bronze suit of armor from Dendra is topped by a boars'-tusk helmet. Such armor was heavy, and soon became obsolete.

Visages of Forgotten Kings

Life-sized face masks of hammered gold accompanied Mycenaean kings when they were interred. Nothing like them has ever been found elsewhere in the Aegean. Heinrich Schliemann unearthed the one on the opposite page and mistakenly identified it as the death mask of the Greek monarch Agamemnon. Actually, it is a likeness of an unknown king who lived some 300 years earlier. But how close a likeness remains a question: Are they true portraits? Comparison of the masks suggests that they were indeed the images of real individuals; there is enough variety in features and expression to justify the conclusion.

This Mycenaean king was a popeyed, round-faced man with a wide, gently smiling mouth.

"Agamemnon" was tight-lipped and straight-nosed. A full but neatly trimmed beard framed his imperious features.

The Emergence of Man

This chart records the progression of life on earth from its first appearance in the warm waters of the new-formed planet through the evolution of man himself; it traces his physical, social, technological and intellectual development to the Christian era. To place these advances in commonly used chronological sequences, the column at the

Geology	Archeology	Billions of Years Ago	
Precambrian earliest era		4.5	Creation of the Earth
		4	Formation of the primordial sea
		3	First life, single-celled algae and bacteria, appears in water
		2	
		1	

		Millions of Years Ago	
			First oxygen-breathing animals appear
		800	
			Primitive organisms develop interdependent specialized cells
		600	Shell-bearing multicelled invertebrate animals appear
Paleozoic ancient life			Evolution of armored fish, first animals to possess backbones
		400	Small amphibians venture onto land
			Reptiles and insects arise
			Thecodont, ancestor of dinosaurs, arises
			Age of dinosaurs begins
Mesozoic middle life		200	Birds appear
			Mammals live in shadow of dinosaurs
			Age of dinosaurs ends
		80	
			Prosimians, earliest primates, develop in trees
Cenozoic recent life		60	
		40	Monkeys and apes evolve
		20	
		10	Ramapithecus, oldest known primate with apparently manlike traits, evolves in India and Africa
		8	
		6	Australopithecus, closest primate ancestor to man, appears in Africa
		4	

Geology	Archeology	Millions of Years Ago	
Lower Pleistocene oldest period of most recent epoch	**Lower Paleolithic** oldest period of Old Stone Age	2	Oldest known tool fashioned by man in Africa
		1	First true man, Homo erectus, emerges in East Indies and Africa
			Homo erectus populates temperate zones

Geology	Archeology	Thousands of Years Ago	
Middle Pleistocene middle period of most recent epoch		800	Man learns to control and use fire
		600	
			Large-scale, organized elephant hunts staged in Europe
		400	Man begins to make artificial shelters from branches
		200	
Upper Pleistocene latest period of most recent epoch	**Middle Paleolithic** middle period of Old Stone Age		Neanderthal man emerges in Europe
		80	
		60	Ritual burials in Europe and Near East suggest belief in afterlife
			Woolly mammoths hunted by Neanderthals in northern Europe
			Cave bear becomes focus of cult in Europe
		40	
	Upper Paleolithic latest period of Old Stone Age		Cro-Magnon man arises in Europe
			Asian hunters cross Bering Land Bridge to populate New World
			Oldest known written record, lunar notations on bone, made in Europe
			Man reaches Australia
			First artists decorate walls and ceilings of caves in France and Spain
		30	Figurines sculpted for nature worship
		20	Invention of needle makes sewing possible
			Bison hunting begins on Great Plains of North America
Holocene present epoch	**Mesolithic** Middle Stone Age	10	Bow and arrow invented in Europe
			Pottery first made in Japan

(Last Ice Age)

▼ Four billion years ago   ▼ Three billion years ago

▲ Origin of the Earth (4.5 billion)   ▲ First life (3.5 billion)

left of each of the chart's four sections identifies the great geo-
gical eras into which the earth's history is divided by scientists,
nile the second column lists the archeological ages of human his-
ry. The key dates in the rise of life and of man's outstanding
complishments appear in the third column (years and events mentioned in this volume of The Emergence of Man appear in bold type).
The chart is not to scale; the reason is made clear by the bar below,
which represents in linear scale the 4.5 billion years spanned by the
chart—on the scaled bar, the portion relating to the total period of
known human existence (far right) is too small to be distinguished.

Geology	Archeology	Years B.C.	
Holocene (cont.)	Neolithic New Stone Age	9000	
			Sheep domesticated in Near East
			Dog domesticated in North America
		8000	Jericho, oldest known city, settled
			Goat domesticated in Persia
			Man cultivates his first crops, wheat and barley, in Near East
		7000	Pattern of village life grows in Near East
			Catal Hüyük, in what is now Turkey, becomes largest Neolithic city
			Loom invented in Near East
			Cattle domesticated in Near East
		6000	Agriculture begins to replace hunting in Europe
	Copper Age		Copper used in trade in Mediterranean area
			Corn cultivated in Mexico
		4800	Oldest known massive stone monument built in Brittany
		4000	Sail-propelled boats used in Egypt
			First city-states develop in Sumer
			Cylinder seals begin to be used as marks of identification in Near East
		3500	First potatoes grown in South America
			Wheel originates in Sumer
			Man begins to cultivate rice in Far East
			Silk moth domesticated in China
			Horse domesticated in south Russia
			Egyptian merchant trading ships start to ply the Mediterranean
			Pictographic writing invented in Near East
	Bronze Age	3000	Bronze first used to make tools in Near East
			City life spreads to Nile Valley
			Plow is developed in Near East
			Accurate calendar based on stellar observation devised in Egypt
		2800	Stonehenge, most famous of ancient stone monuments, begun in England
			Pyramids built in Egypt
		2600	Variety of gods and heroes glorified in Gilgamesh and other epics in Near East

Geology	Archeology	Years B.C.	
Holocene (cont.)	Bronze Age (cont.)	2500	Cities rise in the Indus Valley
			Earliest evidence of use of skis in Scandinavia
			Earliest written code of laws drawn up in Sumer
		2000	Minoan palace societies begin on Crete
			Use of bronze in Europe
			Chicken and elephant domesticated in Indus Valley
			Eskimo culture begins in Bering Strait area
		1500	Invention of ocean-going outrigger canoes enables man to reach islands of South Pacific
			Ceremonial bronze sculptures created in China
			Imperial government, ruling distant provinces, established by Hittites
		1400	Iron in use in Near East
			First complete alphabet devised in script of the Ugarit people in Syria
			Hebrews introduce concept of monotheism
		1000	Reindeer domesticated in Eurasia
	Iron Age		Phoenicians spread alphabet
		900	
		800	Use of iron begins to spread throughout Europe
			First highway system built in Assyria
			Homer composes Iliad and Odyssey
			Mounted nomads appear in the Near East as a new and powerful force
		700	Rome founded
			Wheel barrow invented in China
		200	Epics about India's gods and heroes, the Mahabharata and Ramayana, written
			Water wheel invented in Near East
		0	Christian era begins

▼ Two billion years ago   ▼ One billion years ago

First oxygen-breathing animals (900 million) ▲   First animals to possess ▲   First men (1.3 million) ▲
                                                    backbones (470 million)

Credits

Sources for the illustrations appear below. Credits from left to right are separated by semicolons, from top to bottom by dashes.

Cover—Painting and background photograph by Michael A. Hampshire. 8—Leonard von Matt from Rapho Guillumette. 12, 13 —Map by David Greenspan. 15—Ullstein Bilderdienst, Berlin; The Mansell Collection, London. 17, 18, 19—The Ashmolean Museum, Oxford. 23—Deutsches Archäologisches Institut, Athens. 27—Hirmer Fotoarchiv, Munich. 31 through 37—Renderings by James Alexander. 38—Giraudon courtesy Musée du Louvre, Paris. 40—Hannibal courtesy National Archeological Museum, Athens. 42—Drawing based on Bosert 1967 and Doumas 1963 from The Emergence of Civilisation by Colin Renfrew, Methuen and Co. Ltd., London. 44—Photo Émile courtesy National Archeological Museum, Athens. 47—Staatliche Antikensammlungen und Glyptothek, Munich. 51 through 55—Courtesy National Archeological Museum, Athens. 51, 52, 53 —D. A. Harissiadis. 54—D. A. Harissiadis; A. Stamatopoulos. 55—D. A. Harissiadis. 56 —Giraudon courtesy Archeological Museum, Heraklion, Crete. 58, 59—Leonard von Matt from Rapho Guillumette courtesy Archeological Museum, Heraklion, Crete. 60—C. M. Dixon—Leonard von Matt from Rapho Guillumette courtesy Archeological Museum, Heraklion, Crete. 61—Leonard von Matt from Rapho Guillumette courtesy Archeological Museum, Heraklion, Crete. 63—Orion Press-FPG. 64—C. M. Dixon; C. M. Dixon courtesy Archeological Museum, Heraklion, Crete —Leonard von Matt from Rapho Guillumette. 65—From The Palace of Minos at Knossos by Sir Arthur Evans, Vol. III courtesy Agathon Press, Inc., New York. 68 through 74 except 72—Courtesy Archeological Museum, Heraklion, Crete. 68—C. M. Dixon—Leonard von Matt from Rapho Guillumette. 69—Dan McCoy from Black Star. 70, 71—Leonard von Matt from Rapho Guillumette. 72—Drawing by Adolph E. Brotman. 74—Leonard von Matt from Rapho Guillumette. 76, 77—Michael A. Hampshire; From The Palace of Minos at Knossos by Sir Arthur Evans, Vol. III courtesy Agathon Press, Inc., New York. 78, 79—Adapted by Walter Johnson from The Palace of Minos at Knossos by Sir Arthur Evans, Vol. III courtesy Agathon Press, Inc., New York. 81—Reflejo from Susan Griggs Agency. 82, 83—Maitland A. Edey—From James Walter Graham, The Palace of Crete (copyright © 1962 by Princeton University Press), figure 58, reprinted by permission of Princeton University Press; Leonard von Matt from Rapho Guillumette. 84—Leonard von Matt from Rapho Guillumette. 85—Maitland A. Edey. 86, 87—Maitland A. Edey—From James Walter Graham, The Palace of Crete (copyright © 1962 by Princeton University Press), figure 48, reprinted by permission of Princeton University Press; C. M. Dixon. 88, 89—Maitland A. Edey. 90—Photo J. Ph. Charbonnier, Agence TOP. 92 through 101—Drawings by Michael A. Hampshire. 103, 104, 105—Maitland A. Edey. 106—Left (top and bottom), Maitland A. Edey; Right, Ekdotike Athenon S.A. 109 —Ekdotike Athenon S.A. courtesy National Archeological Museum, Athens. 111 through 119—Courtesy National Archeological Museum, Athens. 111, 112—Dmitri Kessel for the Smithsonian Institution. 113 through 116 —Ekdotike Athenon S.A. 117—Hirmer Fotoarchiv, Munich. 118—Dmitri Kessel for the Smithsonian Institution. 119—Ekdotike Athenon S.A. 120—D. A. Harissiadis. 122—Hirmer Fotoarchiv, Munich courtesy National Archeological Museum, Athens. 125—Top, Leonard von Matt from Rapho Guillumette courtesy Archeological Museum, Heraklion, Crete—Center, photographs by courtesy of the Director of the Archeological Museum, Heraklion, Crete—Bottom, Larry Burrows, from TIME-LIFE Picture Agency, courtesy Archeological Museum, Heraklion, Crete. 127 —The Tourist Photo Library, London. 128 —From The Mycenaean Room in the National Museum, Athens by Alan and Helen Wace, Plate I. Reproduced by permission of Mrs. Alan Wace—Cross section of a tholos tomb based on an original drawing by Alan J. B. Wace from Mycenae, An Archeological History and Guide by Alan J. B. Wace, Biblo and Tannen, New York, 1964. 129—After Hood, Dawn of Civilization, Thames & Hudson Ltd., London and McGraw-Hill Book Co. Inc., New York. 132, 133—Ekdotike Athenon S.A. 134—Deutsches Archäologisches Institut, Athens. 135—From The Minoans by Sinclair Hood, Thames & Hudson Ltd., London. 137—Roger Viollet. 141—French School of Archeology, Athens. 145 through 153 —Courtesy National Archeological Museum, Athens. 145—Hannibal. 146—D. A. Harissiadis. 147—Spyros Tsavdaroglou. 148—D. A. Harissiadis. 149—D. A. Harissiadis—Hannibal—C. M. Dixon. 150—Spyros Tsavdaroglou. 151, 152—D. A. Harissiadis. 153 —C. M. Dixon.

Acknowledgments

For the help given in the preparation of this book, the editors are particularly indebted to Sinclair Hood, archeologist and author, Oxford, England; the late Spyridon N. Marinatos, member of the Academy of Athens, former Inspector General of Antiquities, Greece, and director of excavations at Thera; and George E. Mylonas, member of the Academy of Athens, Professor Emeritus, Washington University, St. Louis, Missouri, and director of excavations at Mycenae, Greece. The editors also express their gratitude to Stylianos E. Alexiou, Director, Archeological Museum, Heraklion, Crete; Ashmolean Museum, Oxford, England; Marlene Barasch, Scarsdale, New York; Catherine Bélanger, Public Relations, Louvre Museum, Paris; H. W. Catling, Director, The British School of Archaeology at Athens; George Dontas, Director, Acropolis Museum, Athens; C. W. J. Eliot, Professor, The American School of Classical Studies at Athens; Max Hirmer, Munich; Lela Karouzo, Athens; Nikolaos Kondoleon, Inspector General of Antiquities, Greece; Doreen Magazian, Athens; James R. McCredie, Director, The American School of Classical Studies at Athens; Marie Montambault, Department of Greek and Roman Antiquities, Louvre Museum, Paris; Efie Sakellarakis, Secretary, the Agora excavation, Athens; J. A. Sakellarakis, Curator of the Prehistoric Collection, National Archeological Museum, Athens; Bernhard Schmalz, The German School of Archeology at Athens; Alkmini Stravridhis, National Archeological Museum, Athens; Dorothy B. Vitaliano, geologist, U.S. Geological Survey, Washington, D.C.; Nikolaos Yalouris, Director, National Archeological Museum, Athens.

Bibliography

Christopoulos, George A., and John Bastias, eds., Prehistory and Protohistory. Translated by Philip Sherrard. Ekdotike Athenon S.A., 1974.

Cottrell, Leonard, The Bull of Minos. Rinehart & Company Inc., 1958.

Edwards, I. E., et al., eds., Cambridge Ancient History, Vol. II, Part 1. History of the Middle East and the Aegean Region, 3rd ed. Cambridge University Press, 1972.

Evans, Arthur, The Palace of Minos at Knossos, Vols. I-IV. Macmillan & Company, Ltd., 1921-1935.

Evans, Joan, Time and Chance: The Story of Arthur Evans and His Forebears. Longmans Green and Co., 1943.

Finley, M. I.:
The Ancient Greeks. Viking Press, 1964.
The World of Odysseus. Viking Press, 1965.

Galanopoulos, A. G., and Edward Bacon, Atlantis: The Truth Behind the Legend. The Bobbs-Merrill Company, 1969.

Graham, James Walter, The Palaces of Crete. Princeton University Press, 1969.

Higgins, Reynold, Minoan and Mycenaean Art. Thames and Hudson, 1967.

Herodotus, The Persian Wars. Translated by

George Rawlinson, *The Greek Historians,* Vol. I. Random House, 1942.

Hood, Sinclair:
The Home of the Heroes: The Aegean before the Greeks. Thames and Hudson, 1967.
The Minoans: Crete in the Bronze Age. Thames and Hudson, 1971.

Hutchinson, R. W., *Prehistoric Crete.* Pelican Books, 1962.

Lattimore, Richmond, trans., *The Iliad of Homer.* University of Chicago Press, 1951.

Luce, J. V., *The End of Atlantis.* Paladin, 1970.

Marinatos, Spyridon:
Excavations at Thera, Numbers 1-6, Athens, 1963-1974.
Life and Art in Prehistoric Thera. Proceedings of the British Academy, Vol. LVII. Oxford University Press, 1971.

Matz, Friedrich, *The Art of Crete and Early Greece.* Crown Publishers, Inc., 1962.

Muhly, James D., "The Hittites and the Aegean World." *Expedition,* Vol. 16, No. 2, Winter, 1974.

Mylonas, George E., *Mycenae and the Mycenaean Age.* Princeton University Press, 1966.

Nilsson, Martin P., *The Minoan-Mycenaean Religion and Its Survival in Greek Religion.* Biblo and Tannen, 1971.

Page, Denys L., *History and the Homeric Iliad.* University of California Press, 1972.

Payne, Robert, *The Gold of Troy.* Funk & Wagnalls, 1959.

Pendlebury, J.D.S., *The Archaeology of Crete.* W. W. Norton & Company, Inc., 1965.

Platon, Nicholas, *Zakros: The Discovery of a Lost Palace of Ancient Crete.* Charles Scribner's Sons, 1971.

Renfrew, Colin:
Before Civilization: The Radiocarbon Revolution and Prehistoric Europe. Alfred A. Knopf, 1967.
The Emergence of Civilisation: The Cyclades and the Aegean in the Third Millennium B.C. Methuen & Co., Ltd., 1972.

Simpson, R. Hope, and J. F. Lazenby, *The Catalogue of Ships in Homer's Iliad.* Clarendon Press, 1970.

Taylour, Lord William, *The Mycenaeans.* Praeger Publishers, 1964.

Thucydides, *The Peloponnesian War.* Translated by Benjamin Jowett, *The Greek Historians,* Vol. I. Random House, 1942.

Vermeule, Emily, *Greece in the Bronze Age.* University of Chicago Press, 1972.

Vitaliano, Dorothy B., *Legends of the Earth.* Indiana University Press, 1973.

Vitaliano, Dorothy B. and Charles J., "Plinian Eruptions, Earthquakes, and Santorin, a Review." Reprinted from the ACTA of the First International Scientific Conference on the Volcano of Thera, 1969.

"Volcanic Tephra on Crete." *American Journal of Archaeology,* Vol. 78, No. 1, January 1974.

Wace, Alan, *Mycenae: An Archaeological History and Guide.* Biblo and Tannen, 1964.

Zervos, Christian, *L'Art des Cyclades.* Editions "Cahiers d'Art," 1957.

Index

Numerals in italics indicate an illustration of the subject mentioned.

Printed in U.S.A. **X**